DIVING AND SNORKELING GUIDE TO

The Best Caribbean Diving

Susanne and Stuart Cummings

Pisces Books®
A division of Gulf Publishing Company
Houston, Texas

Many thanks to the following photographers:

J. Bourque, Frank and Joyce Burek, J. Conklin, K. Greenwood, Greg Johnston, Burt Jones, Bob Keller, Michael Lawrence, J. Leek, Franz Meyer, B. K. Moore, H. Parkey, Carl Roessler, Jim Scheiner, Jerry Schnabel, and Susie Swygert.

Pisces Books®

A division of Gulf Publishing Company
P.O. Box 2608
Houston, Texas 77252-2608

Pisces Books is a registered trademark of Gulf Publishing Company.

Printed in Hong Kong

10   9   8   7   6   5   4   3   2   1

Library of Congress Cataloging-in-Publication Data

Cummings, Susanne.
  Diving and snorkeling guide to the best Caribbean diving /
Susanne and Stuart Cummings.
      p.   cm.
  Includes index.
  ISBN 1-55992-082-3
    1. Deep diving—Caribbean Area—Guidebooks
  2. Snorkeling—Caribbean Area—Guidebooks.   3. Caribbean
  Area—Guidebooks.   I. Cummings, Stuart.   II. Title.
  GV840.S78.C837 1995
  797.2′3—dc20   95-12828
                                                                          CIP

Publisher's note: At the time of publication of this book, all the information was determined to be as accurate as possible. However, when you use this guide, new construction may have changed land reference points, weather may have altered reef configurations, and some businesses may no longer be in operation. Your assistance in keeping future editions up-to-date will be greatly appreciated.

Also, please pay particular attention to depth and bottom time. Know your limits!

Table of Contents

The dark sand of the volcanic sea bottom surrounding Dominica helps to camouflage a resident lobster. (Photo: S. Cummings)

Introduction

The Caribbean has one of the most well-developed and organized dive industries in the world. You can virtually tailor a dive vacation to suit your individual tastes, budget, and diving and snorkeling skills. Some destinations are well-developed with a sophisticated tourist infrastructure offering a wide range of accommodations, dining and entertainment, while others remain sleepy little fishing islands oozing with charm and local color, deserted beaches, and quiet evenings for listening to the waves and crickets. Each island is different and each has a flavor its own. While it is impossible to recommend the best island for your dive vacation—what is paradise to one person may not be to another—it is possible to guide you to the very best diving in the Caribbean.

The purpose of this guide is not to provide you with detailed information on any one destination or dive site, but rather to provide an overview of those Caribbean destinations that top the list of superlative underwater experiences. Unlike other *Pisces Diving and Snorkeling Guides,* there are no ratings in this book. All dive destinations described in this guide merit five stars underwater. Each offers excellent opportunities for divers of all experiences and skill levels. All have received unanimous rave reviews from professional underwater photographers, top dive publications, and numerous experienced divers who have explored the best reefs and walls all over the world. Each offers a distinctive dive experience and a unique islands vacation. Most of them offer such a varied and large marine environment that divers will likely feel compelled to return to the same destination more than once.

As you peruse this guide, most likely you will notice that some of your favorite destinations have been omitted. This guide in no way intends to imply that there are not other islands more than worthy of a visit. The U.S. Virgin Islands, British Virgin Islands, Curacao and Aruba (see page 80), just to name a few, feature some excellent diving and some individual dive sites that rank among the best. But the selections in this guide have been included because the general diving they offer is consistently superb *and* they offer an extraordinary number of dives that are particularly memorable.

So, if you are a new diver who, with all the choices out there, does not know where to begin, or a seasoned diver looking for something new, challenging and spectacular, this guide is for you. Choose your destination for the underwater or topside characteristics, or visit them all! They should keep you in warm water for years to come!

1

The Bahamas

The Bahamas is not a diving destination, it is a diving dynasty. With 700 islands spread over 100,000 square miles of ocean, the Bahamas actually comprise 25 different diving destinations featuring more than 1,000 distinct dives. So when they promise something for everyone, they are not exaggerating.

Three important features of the area play an influential role in making the Bahamas one of the most diverse and exciting regions in the Caribbean. The Gulf Stream is a source of clear, clean water that keeps the coral reefs pristine and healthy while it also prevents the islands from the rain and runoff from the Florida coast. The Bahamas Trenches also carry clear water to the area and provide a very deep receptacle for any sediment that might otherwise settle on the reefs. Finally, the Bahamas Banks serve as a breeding ground for a wide variety of marine life. The result is a crystal clear view of an abundance of fish and corals.

There is unlimited world-class diving that should be enough to attract divers to these islands, but the Bahamas offers some unique underwater adventures found in few other places—shark diving and dolphin encounters!

Harbour Island offers out-island vistiors a tranquil ambiance and picturesque scenery. (Photo: S. Cummings)

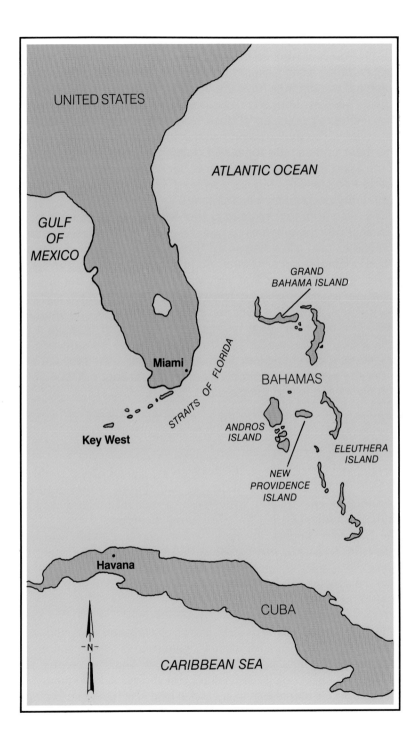

3

Dolphin Encounters

Have you ever noticed that dolphins always seem to be laughing? And they always seem to be playing games. On a Caribbean dolphin dive, you may have the opportunity to join in the fun and absorb quite an education about dolphin behavior at the same time. Although you can choose one of the controlled dolphin encounters, the thrill of diving with wild dolphins is unparalleled. The most popular site for a wild dolphin encounter is along the White Sand Ridge on the Bahamas Bank where resident pods of spotted dolphins are regularly sighted. These dolphins definitely control the encounters with humans.

You have front row seats to one of Mother Nature's finest performances as the dolphins forage, feed, and play with each other sometimes only a few feet away. Summertime is the best season for encounters because the dolphins make an appearance almost every day. Your first sighting is likely to be at the bow of your boat as the dolphins catch the wake for a little body surfing. Once you've found the pod, you can enter the water on snorkel, which the dolphins seem to prefer over scuba. If they want to play, they'll come to you. The dolphins seem to be attracted to swimmers and snorkelers who imitate their own movements under the water. So spend a little time snorkeling, practice your free diving and join in the games!

The Bahamas is definitely the shark diving capital of the world with more than 60,000 divers to date having participated in organized shark dives throughout the islands. While these encounters are conducted in an organized and safe way, the "rush" is unforgettable.

The Bahamas dolphin diving is world renowned with two superb opportunities to interact one on one with Atlantic bottlenose and spotted dolphins. These are truly close encounters. Divers beware. These dolphins display a distinct preference for humans who breath more like they do— through snorkels!

New Providence Island is best known among most travelers as the home of Nassau and Paradise Islands, glittering vacation paradise with 400 banks, British colonial architecture, elegant homes, duty-free shopping, fabulous resort hotels, casinos, cabaret shows, and enormous cruise ship docks. To the surprise of many, this island also has a laid-back quiet side to it—the **South Side**—where pine trees and exquisite uncrowded white sand beaches dominate the landscape.

The shallow waters of the Devil's Backbone are ideal for divers and snorkelers alike, but the reefs have been treacherous for passing ships for centuries. (Photo: S. Cummings)

The quiet, uncrowded beaches of New Providence Island in the Bahamas offer a restful alternative to the casinos and busy shopping markets. (Photo: S. Cummings)

The underwater environment around this island is as diverse as the island's topside. Wrecks, blue holes, and shark dives only hint at the world below the surface, and most sites are within 30 minutes by boat.

Cool Dives: Lost Blue Hole, Fish Hotel, Barracuda Shoals, The Graveyard, the Mahoney wrecks, Shark Wall, Shark Buoy, Bond Wrecks, Tunnel Wall, Southwest Reef, and Goulding Cay.

Hot Sightings: Blue holes more than 100 feet in diameter, Nassau groupers, sergeant majors, moray eels, soft corals, sea fans, juvenile grunts, goatfish, trumpetfish, lots of wrecks, Caribbean Reef sharks, dolphinfish, jacks, rainbow runners, silky sharks, water visibility typically in excess of 150 feet; wrecks used for Hollywood sets, gorgonians, sponges, crevices, tunnels, elkhorn and staghorn coral, squirrelfish, barracuda.

Super snorkels: Goulding Cay.

The second most popular island among tourists is **Grand Bahama Island.** In both **Freeport** and **Lucaya,** golf courses, resort hotels, casinos, duty-free shopping, and the full range of tropical watersports are readily available to entertain visitors.

The shallow waters of the Bahamas Bank combined with a healthy mangrove system along the shore is a productive marine nursery. This is complemented by two deep chasms with extraordinary visibility and pelagic activity to provide divers with a full range of dive opportunities. The highlight for many visiting divers is the close encounter with bottlenose dolphins.

Cool Dives: Theo's Wreck, Shark Junction, Tunnels, Pygmy Caves, Ben's Caverns.

Hot Sightings: Turtles, horse-eye jacks, spotted and green moray eels, bottlenose dolphin, Caribbean Reef sharks, swim-throughs, schools of jacks, mutton snappers, yellowtails, caves and caverns, submerged stalactites and stalagmites.

If **Nassau** and **Freeport** represent the glitter and sizzle of the Bahamas, the **out islands** are the epitome of tranquil seclusion and unspoiled nature at its best. The Out Islands are to many, the real treasure of the Bahamas.

The **Abacos**—including **Marsh Harbour, Green Turtle Cay** and **Walker's Cay, Bimini,** and **Andros**—extend from Walker's Cay at the northern end 130 miles to the southern end of Great Abaco. The area including Marsh Harbour, Green Turtle Cay, and Walker's Cay, is a premiere sailing destination. But it also holds some excellent surprises for divers. A marine park protects the easy shallow sites with elegant pillar coral, large pinnacles, tunnels and caverns, and prolific sea life. The northernmost island, Walker's Cay, features all types of diving from a fabulous shark dive to drop-offs, and fringing and patch reefs with an abundance of marine activity and heavy, thick coral formations.

◀ *The international straw market in Freeport is one of the most popular duty-free shopping emporia in the Bahamas. (Photo: S. Cummings)*

Cool Dives: The Towers, Grouper Alley, Wayne's World, The Cathedral, Tarpon Reef, Coral Caverns, *San Jacinto* Wreck, The Catacombs, Coral Condos, Spiral Cavern, Pirates' Cathedral, Barracuda Alley, Shark Rodeo (100 sharks and 100 groupers); Shark Canyon.

Hot Sightings: School of tarpon, huge green moray, winding caverns, shiny silversides, turtles, cascading plate coral.

Bimini is synonymous with fish. Essentially patch reefs, this island has no rival in sheer quantity of marine creatures, both reef fish and ocean pelagics. This is where you'll consistently see clouds of fish from schooling grunts and chub to snapper and goatfish. But there is also variety, and standard underwater fare includes spotted eagle rays, nurse sharks, turtles, prolific live corals, colorful sponge formations with plenty of photo ops.

Cool Dives: Bimini Barge, The Victories, Tuna Alley, Little Caverns, Rainbow Reef.

Diving with the Sharks!

There are generally two kinds of divers—those who are terrified by the thought of coming face to face with a shark underwater—and those who relish the prospect. For the latter group, dive operators in several Caribbean destinations can guarantee an authentic shark encounter of the photogenic kind! For 30 to 40 minutes, you can observe the behavior of as many as 20 sharks—including Caribbean reef, lemon, bull, and silky sharks—as they circle above and in front of you sometimes only 20 feet away. On a very rare occasion, a hammerhead may even make an appearance!

The shark dives are well-organized and quite safe for divers with an experienced dive master controlling the dive and keeping the attention of the incredible creatures concentrated on himself. In the Bahamas alone, more than 60,000 divers have participated in shark dives with no incidents of injury.

Although divers are asked to refrain from swimming around, underwater photography and video enthusiasts will have ample opportunity to bring home some unbelievable images. And don't imagine that if you've seen one, you've seen them all. In the Bahamas, for example, eight different dive operators in different parts of the region offer shark dives. Each experience is distinctive and each is equally capable of increasing your heart and air consumption rate!

Great Inagua plays host to a huge community of pink flamingos. (Photo: S. Cummings)

Andros, the largest of the islands and one of least explored dive environments, is situated alongside a 120-mile barrier reef, the third longest in the world. The outside of the reef plunges thousands of feet into The Tongue of the Ocean, creating fabulous walls. Inside the reef, you'll find shallow blue holes, shipwrecks surrounded by beautiful coral gardens, and spur and groove reef formations punctuated by large pinnacles.

Cool Dives: Over the Wall, Edge of the Wall, Giant Staircase, Gardens, Marion.

Hot Sightings: Wrecks, schools of grouper, snappers, and giant rainbow parrotfish.

Unlike Andros, **Eleuthera** is one of best developed and most prosperous of the out-islands, although no less picturesque with its pink sand beaches, rolling hills, and dramatic cliffs. Diving occurs on the long fringing reef that borders Eleuthera and adjacent **Harbour Island.** Nearby **Spanish Wells** also abuts another long fringing reef. These reefs are unspoiled, revealing beautiful displays of star, starlet and plate coral, a good variety of reef and pelagic fish and lots of wrecks along Devil's Backbone.

Cool Dives: Devil's Backbone, Plateau, Arch, Current Cut, Pinnacles, Eleuthera Train Wreck, Carnavon Wreck.

Hot Sightings: Ancient and modern wrecks, patch reefs, schools of grunts, snappers and horse-eye jacks, eagle rays, giant sponges, black coral.

A friendly yellow coney conveniently pauses on the reef to pose for a photographer's camera. (Photo: S. Cummings)

◄ *Elephant ears sponges grow to a huge size in the clear, clean waters of the Bahamas. (Photo: S. Cummings)*

San Salvador, the epitome of the "out-island", is the land of the vertical walls. One of first destinations to develop wall diving, San Sal still attracts divers' attention with on of the most stunning walls in the Bahamas. The shallow reefs also team with fish and invertebrate life, ideal for macro photographers.

Cool Dives: Telephone Pole, Snapshot Reef, Devil's Claw, Great Cut, Double Caves.

Hot Sightings: Gregarious groupers, manta rays, hammerhead sharks and other big ocean critters.

Not too many divers make it to **Long Island,** but those who do discover an undisturbed hideaway that hasn't been altered by time. Long Island's Shark Reef was one of the earliest organized shark dives and set the standard for shark encounters around the world. Nassau groupers spawn here in November and there is a good chance of seeing pelagics.

Cool Dives: Barracuda Heads, wreck of the Comberbach, Grouper Valley, Conception Island, Southampton Reef.

Hot Sightings: Schooling horse-eye jacks, grunts, barracuda, schools of Nassau grouper, walls beginning in 40 feet and dropping over to more than 6,000, elkhorn and staghorn coral on at least 150 wrecks.

For the truly adventurous, the **southern Bahamas** is virtually undiscovered by mainstream tourism, although it is a haven for eco-tourists and divers. The farther south you go, the wilder and more natural the islands become. That isn't to say there is no sign of human civilization—**Conception, Rum Cay, the Exumas, Samana Cay, Mayaguana,** and **Great** and **Little Inagua** serve as staging areas for accessing the superb and almost limitless diving adventures. Amid some of the lushest coral gardens and walls in the Caribbean populated by thousands of multi-hued fish of every local species and size, divers will be able to observe fish cleaning stations, mating rituals, and predatory behavior "up close and personal."

Cool Dives: Elkhorn Gardens of the Exumas, The Exuma National Land and Sea Park, a 22-mile-long park, 176 square miles of island and sea bottom, vast underwater preserve offering shallow reefs, blue holes, drop-offs, and cave and cavern dives, Conception Island Wall, Snowfields at Rum Cay, Angelfish Blue Hole, Crab Cay Crevasse, Lobster Reef, Pagoda Reef, Stingray Reef, Crooked Island Drop-Off, Ragged Island Fringing Reef, Hogsty Reef, Great Inagua Wall.

Hot Sightings: Blue holes, rays, sharks, dolphins, whales, lobster, schooling fish, invertebrates of all kinds.

If you happen to be in the Bahamas around the New Year, visit Nassau for Junkanoo, the Bahamians' version of Mardi Gras, is one of the most colorful and celebrated festivals in the Caribbean.

Costumes, three or more times the size of a man, colorfully portray the theme of the Junkanoo parade. Each costume must be entirely supported by one individual.
(Photo: B. Keller)

◄ At Hogsty Reef, virgin reefs flourish undisturbed by any outside influences.
(Photo: S. Cummings)

2

Bay Islands

Some places never change. Those divers who discovered the Bay Islands years ago and still return to this quiet laid-back dive destination wouldn't want it any other way. The Bay Islands have not lost their Caribbean charm, nor have their healthy underwater reef formations and walls diminished in lushness, size, or magnificence. This marine environment remains a very impressive sight.

Topside, the Bay Islands are still slow paced and uncrowded, another area resort developers have overlooked. Only in recent years have the Bay Islands begun promoting tourism and diving, perfectly attuned to the emergence of the eco-tourism concept. The result has been greater awareness of the islands among travelers and greater appreciation of the wonders of the natural environment.

The Bay Islands consist of three large islands, three smaller ones, and about 60 islets and cays situated just off the Caribbean coast of Honduras. They are part of a submerged volcanic ridge that extends offshore from the Sierra de Omoa mountain range.

Topside, the Bay Islands offer the classic image of the tropical Caribbean, richly swathed in a multi-hued green jungle that cascades down to a turquoise and deep blue sea, rich in natural treasures of its own. During one of his exploratory journeys, Christopher Columbus appropriately chose the name Honduras or "deep sea" for the sheer drop-offs near the shore on both sides of the islands. Wall-diving enthusiasts will be in their element because these drop-offs begin as shallow as 40 feet and almost every dive site has a wall dive. But the reefs are also extraordinary.

The Bay Islands share the same barrier reef system that passes by Cozumel and Belize, as well as the typically large reef formations and shallow steep walls. Sixty-five species of hard corals complemented by an impressive selection of sponges, sea fans, sea whips, and gorgonians grace the reefs. Reef fish are always out in force, joining the occasional ocean pelagic on the outside walls.

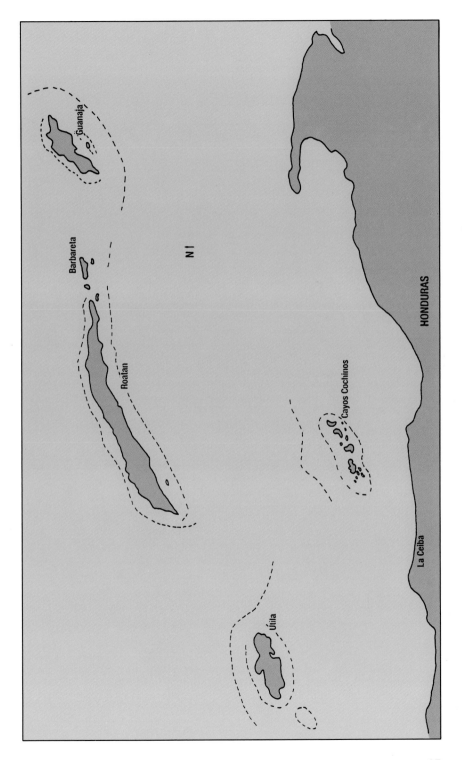

Guanaja

Barbareta

N I

Roatán

Cayos Cochinos

HONDURAS

Utila

La Ceiba

15

Stunning sunsets cast a golden glow over the water in Roatan. (Photo: G. Johnston)

◄ *At "West End" in the Bay Islands, lush growth of sponges of every kind and size decorate the reefs. (Photo: G. Johnston)*

Roatan is the largest of the Bay Islands. It is the most populous of the islands and the most developed in terms of tourism including the number of established dive resorts.

The Roatan reefs are notorious for their immense coral formations, impressive by any standards. A vast array of sponges and hard and soft corals blanket huge coral heads, and excellent displays of pillar coral can be found on the shallow reefs. The Bartlett Trough, which is several thousand feet deep, borders Roatan's reef system and the expansive drop-off creates excellent and abundant wall diving. Deep cuts through the coral enable divers to swim through the reefs down to walls covered with large, colorful sponge growth.

Most of the diving around Roatan takes place along an extensive fringing reef that runs along the northern and southern shores and is largely protected by a marine park program. Roatan leads the way in the Bay Islands with the most permanent moorings. Along the northern coast, the barrier reef is almost unbroken while the southern coast features a series of bays sheltered by the fringing reef. For adventurous diving and sightings of large schools of fish, head for the west end.

Cool Dives: Mary's Place, Insidious Reef, Enchanted Forest, West End Wall, Connie's Dream, Romeo's Elbow, Calvin's Crack, Valley of the

17

Several species of hamlets frequent the reefs around the islands. (Photo: S. Cummings)

It is not uncommon to see gray angelfish, often swimming in pairs, cruising along the reefs. (Photo: S. Cummings) ▶

Kings, Prince Albert Shipwreck, Half Moon Bay, Peter's Place, Bear's Den, Mandy's Eel Garden, Pablo's Place,

Hot Sightings: Nudibranchs, octopuses, sea hares, sea horses, frogfish, tunicates, rock hinds, small tiger groupers, angelfish, parrotfish, schools of blue tangs, blue chromis, creole wrasse, buff tube sponges, black coral fans, azure vase sponges and yellow gorgonians.

The last island in the chain, **Guanaja** reaches the tallest elevations at 1,700 feet above sea level. With its looming mountains, a fringe of palm trees circling the coastline and hills covered in pine trees, Guanaja is the essence of a tropical paradise. With only three small villages, an airstrip, and small runabouts and water taxis for transportation around the island, you can't get much farther away from the madding crowds of the civilized world.

Although the islands are quite close, underwater, Guanaja is notably different from Roatan. On the outside of the barrier reef that runs parallel to the northern shore, the vertical walls begin as shallow as 15 feet. On the inside, patch reefs display lavish coral gardens; pinnacles, caverns, and ship wrecks, including one large one, decorate the varied reef areas.

Cool Dives: Jado Trader wreck, Jim's Silverlode, Bayman Drop, Black Rock Canyon, Devil's Cauldron.

Hot Sightings: Elkhorn coral, purple tunicates, reef fish, morays, groupers, turtles, resident jewfish, barracudas.

Barbareta is a private island with gentle hills and perfect beaches lined with palm trees that make it look like a picture postcard. Even if you aren't staying on the island, you can take day-trips to explore **Barbareta Wall,** a drop-off decorated with basket and barrel sponges that extends along the island's southern shore for about a mile. Another site worth visiting is **Pigeon Cays,** great for snorkeling as well as diving.

A green jewel set in turquoise waters, Guanaja boasts breathtaking views from any vantage point (Photo: K. Greenwood)

The striking blue and purple hues of the creole wrasse add a touch of vibrant color to the reef scene. (Photo: S. Cummings)

One small Bay Island, **Utila,** deserves mention because more whale sharks have been spotted near this island than in any other area of Bay Islands.

So far, the Bay Islands have avoided heavy tourism development, maintaining an easy paced, laid back atmosphere, uncrowded topside and underwater. Most of the activity in these islands centers around the charming resorts, although Roatan does have several good restaurants and shops, where visitors seeking souvenirs can find local crafts, carvings, and shells.

Getting to the Bay islands isn't as easy as some dive destinations, but the extra effort and air time is well worth the ultimate reward when you arrive. Here the flavor of the Caribbean is at its purest, and nature still prevails over man.

3

Belize

On the Caribbean coast of Central America just south of the Mexican Yucatan lies the country of Belize. Unlike many Caribbean dive destinations, Belize is not an island but a part of the mainland. Its rich rainforest is renowned among naturalists for its 4,000 species of native flowering plants, including 250 species of orchids and 700 species of native trees, 550 species of birds—more than are found anywhere else in North America—and its being the last refuge of the largest cat found in the western hemisphere, the jaguar. The Belizians are among the most conservation minded of their neighbors, in the vanguard of Central America's eco-tourism industry. But their concern for their environment and natural resources extends beyond the rainforests to include the extensive reef system that runs along the coast of Belize. It is not just any reef they're intent on protecting. At 180 miles in length, it is the second longest barrier reef system in the world and the longest in the Western Hemisphere.

If that is not impressive enough, it is the site of 200 offshore cayes and three of the four atolls to be found in the Caribbean. Just offshore of the mainland, the waters are muddied from the runoff from rain-fed rivers. But along the Barrier Reef 7 to 25 miles offshore, the water is crystal clear.

Offshore there are more than 450 cayes, islets, and islands along the barrier reef that runs from Ambergris Caye in the north to Laughing Bird Caye at its southernmost point. It is around the offshore atolls, a collection of picture postcard tropical islets with fringing sand beaches and clear aqua waters, that the diving is at its best.

The best of Belizian diving is situated off the atolls of **Turneffe, Lighthouse, Half Moon** and **Glover's Cayes.** Because the barrier reef is also the rim of the continental shelf, wall diving is at its best in Belize. Most walls begin in fairly shallow water—20–40 feet—before dropping off. The combination of shallow and deep-water opportunities is ideal for repetitive diving. Divers usually have the opportunity to choose between exploring the top reef areas or heading straight off the vertical precipices.

Turneffe Island Lodge gives divers easy access to world class reefs from Cay Bokel. (Photo: H. Parkey) ▶

Belize forms part of the coast of the Western Caribbean Sea between Mexico and Honduras.

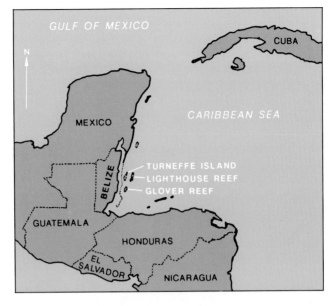

Belize diving means walls crowded with colorful sponges, corals, and rich invertebrate and fish life because of the exposure to open sea and protection provided by the lush reef growth. (Photo: B. Jones)

Large heads and platy growths of boulder coral form the main framework of the reefs. (Photo: F. Burek) ▶

Although many of the sites have similar components—lush coral heads separated by sand chutes on the top reef often forming a labyrinth that divers can swim through as they approach the vertical wall—there is a lot of variety in the configuration of the sites and the marine life.

The largest of the more than 200 cayes that stretch along the coast of Belize is **Ambergris Caye,** a laidback island with charming resorts and "fishing village" ambiance. With the barrier reef only a half-mile offshore, the corals are dense and close to the surface. There are more than 40 sites along the reef that dive operators visit regularly.

Cool Dives: Mexico Rocks, Caverns, Palmetto Reef, Sandy Point and Hol Chan Marine Park.

Hot Sightings: Spur and groove coral formations with cuts, fissures, swim-throughs and walls, tube sponges, deep-water sea fans, sea whips, sea fingers, coral gardens, schools of copper sweepers and Glassy Minnows, lots of tame fish.

Super Snorkel: Mexico Rocks.

At night, the reef octopus searches for a preferred dish of mollusks on the reef at Silver Caves. (Photo: J. Leek)

Belize's three unique atolls offer ideal diving conditions with a reef fringed lagoon and surrounding sheer drop-off, clear waters, and a leeward side that offers divers a calm place to explore.

Turneffe Island Atoll is the closest to Belize City. Once a fisherman's haven for tarpon, bonefish, permit, and wahoo, it was later discovered by divers for the same abundant marine environment.

An extensive mangrove system acts as a nursery for the coral reef life. Rich nutrients are then carried with the outgoing tides to the outside reefs. Visibility may vary with the winds and tides, but the fish activity everywhere is unbelievable.

One hundred dive sites offer divers of all experience levels everything from shallow coral reefs and deep pinnacles to steep walls and wrecks. The fish life is substantial with medium and large reef fish, ocean pelagics, and the miraculous sight of groupers by the thousands spawning.

Cool Dives: Gorgonian Bluff, Black Forest, Cabbage Patch, The Elbow, Myrtle's Turtles and Triple Anchors.

Hot Sightings: Groupers spawning, deep-water gorgonians, black coral, schooling grunts and snapper, elkhorn coral, eagle rays, schools of horse-eye jacks, dog snapper, permits, sea turtles, nurse sharks, green morays, even spotted dolphins.

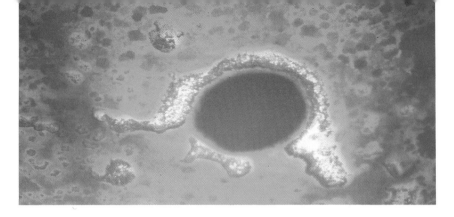

A shallow reef virtually encloses the circular patch of dark blue water that marks Blue Hole. (Photo: F. Meyer)

From the air, **Lighthouse Reef Atoll** is a beautiful sight to divers with its fringing coral that girds a turquoise lagoon, and a clear and colorful drop-off on the outside. It's obvious even from above that the visibility will be spectacular. A closer look will not disappoint as exquisite reef formations and walls that begin as shallow as 35 feet, draped with sponges and corals, appear with superior clarity underwater.

If you are visiting Lighthouse Reef, you won't want to miss a dive at the famous **Blue Hole,** a unique experience as you descend into a perfectly round, roofless cave 1,000 feet across that descends more than 400 feet

Blue Holes

The Blue Hole in Belize is the most famous in the Caribbean, but it is by no means the only one. There are small and large blue holes scattered all over the Caribbean. Some are accessible from land, while others can only be reached by boat. Usually surrounded by relatively shallow reef, from the air they present an impressive vision—perfect circles of deep blue set against pale aquamarine coral reefs.

The blue holes are usually the result of a geological fluke of nature. They are caverns, caves, or sinkholes of varying size and depth that were formed when the level of the ocean was much lower. Over the millennia, the water rose to cover the enclosed pockets in the earth. Eventually, the weight and pressure of the water collapsed the slowly eroding roof to expose the deep abyss below.

Like caves on land, blue holes are often filled with stalagmites and stalactites delicately painted in the colors of encrusting corals and sponges. Blue holes may not offer the prolific marine life of the surrounding reefs, but the sensation of submerging into a huge blue cavern is something unusual!

deep. Dives are generally limited to 130 feet depending on your dive operator. The shallow reefs that surround Blue Hole are full of marine activity. Macro photographers will have a hey-day. Between the atoll and nearby cayes, there are more than 40 sites to explore.

Cool Dives: The Pinnacle, Captain's Choice, East Side Wall, Blue Hole, Cabata, The Aquarium.

Hot Sightings: Black coral, groupers spawning, colorful sponges and corals, hawksbill turtles, trunkfish.

Named for the pirate, John Glover, **Glover's Reef** lies the farthest south of the coral atolls. Twenty-seven dive sites dot the more than 30 miles of fringing reef and feature walls beginning in only 30 feet and plunging to 2,000 feet, deep pinnacles, drift dives, and visibility to 200 feet.

Glovers Reef's distance from Belize City or the other resort islands makes it a less frequently visited dive area. But the southern part of Belize is virtually uncharted virgin territory, so it takes a little more planning and creativity to organize an excursion but for divers who relish adventure, this is it!

Cool Dives: Pinnacles, Masada, Barrel Head, Gorgonia Gallery.

Hot Sightings: Magnificent spur and groove reef formations; top reefs lush with corals and sponges; walls with deep red rope sponges, purple, yellow, and brown giant tube sponges; black coral trees; angelfish, butterflyfish, spotted eagle rays; big nurse sharks; baracudas; schools of tarpon, turtles, stingrays, and even an occasional manta ray.

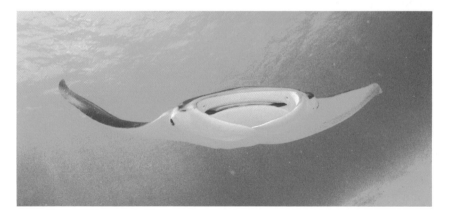

With their cavernous mouths open, manta rays frequently make feeding runs for plankton above the shallow turtle grass flats behind the reef rim at Half Moon Cay. (Photo: B. K. Moore)

◄ *An orange sponge provides a soft resting spot for a sleepy graysby at night. (Photo: J. Burek)*

Some live-aboards feed the fish at Que Brada and divers entering or exiting the water may find themselves surrounded by yellowtail snappers eager for a handout.

◄ *The beauty of Half Moon Caye reefs is now protected thanks to recent adoption of a natural resources management program. Much support and direction came from CEDAM International and its members who did detailed surveys needed for monitoring diver stress on this popular reef. (Photo: J. Conklin)*

Surface Intervals: Half Moon Caye, a photogenic island replete with lighthouse, palm trees, and a booby watching tower. On the mainland, the zoo near Belize City, the Maya ruins at Xunantunich and Altun Ha, the howler monkey refuge known as the Bermudian Landing Community Baboon Sanctuary, Cockscomb Basin Jaguar Preserve. There is even a very plush "spa" in the middle of the jungle.

4

Bonaire

Bonaire is one of the few places in the Caribbean—and maybe in the world—where you can find excellent boat diving, shore diving, and snorkeling all in one place. The consummate dedicated divers' island, Bonaire is a destination where everything from Mother Nature to the local dive operators all happily conspire to spoil divers so that they not only want to return again, but want to bring their friends with them.

Natural weather and water conditions make the island, which is located only 50 miles off the coast of Venezuela and outside the Caribbean Hurricane Belt, an appealing dive destination year-round. Sunshine is the rule of thumb with gentle trade winds keeping the temperatures around 82°F. There is little rainfall to run-off into the surrounding waters, so the waters are generally clear and visibility is consistently good to excellent. Most of the dive sites are located on the western shore of the island protected by the lee so the waters are calm. In other words, this is diving not only at its best but at its most convenient and easiest.

It is next to impossible to resist the allure of Bonaire's calm, clear seas and the wealth of marine activity that awaits below the surface. When Triton calls, divers are invariably overwhelmed by the urge to seek out the nearest dive operation . . . and there is always one nearby.

Divers will observe that Bonaire's government, dive operators, and resorts are very protective of their marine environment. This active involvement began over 30 years ago, long before reef preservation was fashionable, and is largely responsible for the good condition of the reefs.

Bonaire Marine Park encompasses the reefs and walls that surround Bonaire and **Klein Bonaire.** Within the boundaries of the park, spearfishing, collecting, littering, and damaging the reef by touching the corals in any way is strictly taboo. On the last item, buoyancy control workshops are offered as a courtesy by many of the dive operators who feel that good divers are less of a threat to the health of the reefs. These courses are also a lot of fun and guaranteed to improve the diving skills of the even the most seasoned diver.

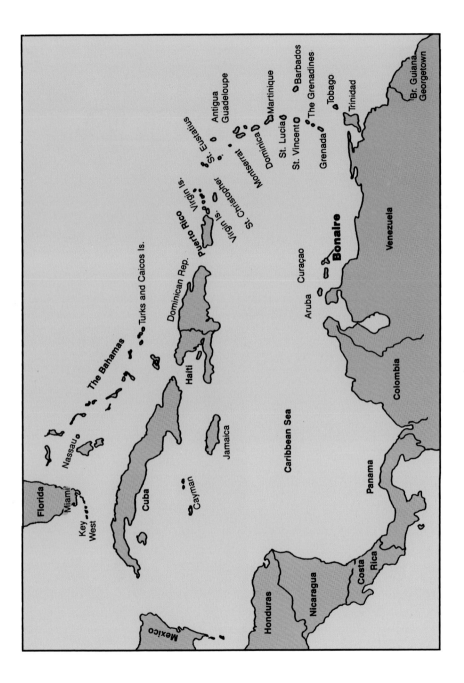

Colorful Dutch architecture is characteristic of the many government and commercial buildings in Bonaire. (Photo: S. Swygert)

Friendly Bonaireans will be glad to show you how to enjoy the latest watersports equipment available at many hotels. (Photo: J. Schnabel) ▶

A blazing sunset enhances this seaside dining experience. Bonaire has an excellent assortment of restaurants to choose from. (Photo: J. Schnabel)

Anchoring on the reef is, of course, prohibited. The comprehensive buoy system along Bonaire's shores is extensive and impressive. The first buoy was installed in 1962. Today, more than 70 buoys at any one time mark dive sites in the marine park. Dive boats must use the buoys, which helps prevent damage to the reefs by anchors, limits the number of divers on a site at one time, and enables the marine park to "close" certain dive sites for periods of time to give them time to rejuvenate.

Another distinctive feature of diving in Bonaire is the quantity and quality of shore diving. Not to say that the walls that are only a five-minute boat ride are not very enticing, but it is the only island in the Caribbean where divers can grab a tank and walk off the beach to equally excellent dive sites that include everything from walls to reefs and even wrecks only a few steps from the beach.

In typical Bonaire style, all of the dive sites have been given names (which all the dive operators have agreed upon) and numbers. Dive site maps and guide books that provide an excellent and detailed source for locations and descriptions of a large selection of the best sites in Bonaire are readily available to visitors. (As with any of the destinations in this guide, Pisces has a specific guide to this location.)

All of the diving around Bonaire is conveniently located all along the calm lee coast from the southern end of the island to the northern end,

The reef begins just a few feet from shore, and the clear and warm water invites snorkelers. Fish feeding is a favorite activity. (Photo: J. Schnabel)

The delightful lined sea horse (Hippocampus erectus) is truly one of the signatures of Bonaire; although sea horses are common, they are hard to find as they blend in so well with their habitat. (Photo: S. Swygert) ▶

around the 1,500-square-acre circular island of **Klein Bonaire** or in **Washington Park,** at the northern top of the island.

You will discover a wide variety and certainly no shortage of outstanding dive and snorkel sites. Reef and wall profiles range from gently terraced slopes that begin at the shore to sharply vertical drop-offs that start in water as shallow as 15 feet. Soft corals and sponges dominate many of the wall dives while areas like Washington Park offer an excellent display of dense and varied hard corals. Colorful tropical fish abound. And, of course, Bonaire is renowned for its small macro creatures.

Cool Dives: Red Slave, Hilma Hooker, Town Pier, Forest, Southwest Corner, Munk's Haven, Front Porch, Rappel, Boca Slagbaai, Playa Funchi, Playa Benge.

Hot Sightings: Soft corals, sea fans, deep sea gorgonians and tube sponges everywhere, trumpetfish, filefish, black durgeons, turtles, wrecks with schools of glass minnows and lots of macro critters, frogfish, purple stove pipe sponges, large orange elephant ear sponges, azure vase sponges, schools of creole wrasse, angelfish, groupers, blue tangs, parrotfish. Get your cameras ready!

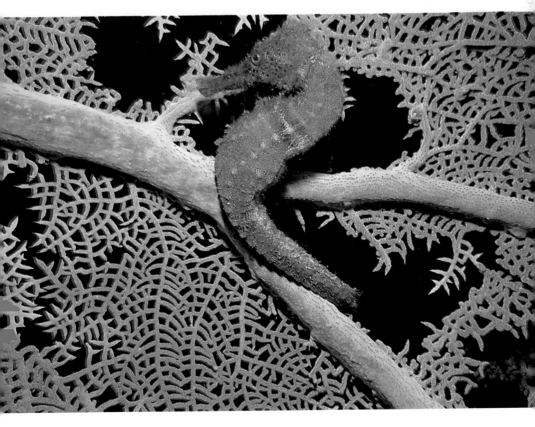

Night Diving at the Piers

The bottom may be littered with soda cans and old tires and the sound of engines continually pierce the tranquillity of the quiet water. It's the place where trash and traffic prevail, but there's nothing like an old pier to attract small marine activity and no place better to shoot macro photography. Piers all over the Caribbean have always attracted divers who congregate in the shallow, critter-filled waters at night when the resident marine community comes out in full force. Bonaire's two piers are among the very best for night diving and an excellent example of how one person's old pilings and garbage can be another person's paradise.

At first glance from the surface, Bonaire's Town Pier and Custom Pier don't look like appealing dive sites, especially after sundown. But with the assistance of a good dive light, the darkness reveals a vivid tapestry of brilliant red, purple, and yellow encrusting sponges, orange tubastrea in full bloom, and mini-anemones, including such rare species as orange and white ball anemones. Fish and invertebrates abound on these relatively limited surfaces. If you look closely you'll see everything from sea horses, frogfish, and decorator crabs to squid, octopus and tiny bejeweled shrimp.

Photographers will find more subjects to capture on celluloid on the piers than on any other single reef or wall dive. And because the depth is shallow, bottom time is substantial. You'll run out of film before you run out of air or time. If you put the pier dives on your dive schedule, do it at the beginning of your dive trip. The chances are that one dive won't be enough!

Be sure to check with the Harbor Master for permission to dive at your proposed time as well as for ship movements around the piers.

You can select any number of dives around Bonaire and Klein Bonaire and get a taste of typical Bonaire diving, but there is only one **Town Pier** and one **Customs Pier.** They are probably Bonaire's most popular dives and certainly the most memorable, especially for macro photographers. Colorful encrusting sponges have turned the pilings into works of modern art as well as a home for tiny fish and invertebrates. This is a good place to see a prolific marine community in 20 feet of water or less and you might even find the resident sea horses, a rare and rewarding experience for any diver.

Piers and wrecks can form a basis for an artifical reef. The Salt Pier pilings are densely covered with an amazing variety of colorful sponges and corals, and many invertebrates shelter among the growth. (Photo: J. Schnabel) ▶

No dive vacation to Bonaire could be complete without a night dive at the famous Town Pier. The flowerlike polyps of the tube corals are extended for nighttime feeding and resemble vivid yellow bouquets. (Photo: S. Swygert)

Although Bonaire has earned a widespread reputation among divers, it is also beginning to emerge as a superb snorkeling destination. The clear, calm waters make snorkeling an effortless activity, ideal for beginners and children due to the conditions, but exciting even for diehard divers due to the prolific marine environment in some of the shallower sites.

Along the coasts of Bonaire and Klein Bonaire, the reefs slope very gradually from the shore before the wall drops off. These shallow waters not only offer snorkelers more than a passing glimpse of the full range of tropical fish but, in some areas, expansive arrays of stunning elkhorn, staghorn, and finger coral.

While several dive sites are also suitable for snorkeling, there are also a number of sites unexplored by divers because they are too shallow for scuba. However, snorkelers will find a wealth of sea life just beneath the surface.

Super Snorkels: Munk's Haven, Carl's Hill, Lenora's Reef, La Machaca, Cliff, Ol' Blue, Boca Bartol, Wayaca, Jeff Davis Reef, Nukove, English Gardens South.

Pelagics occasionally make an appearance out of the blue, but usually there is so much activity on the reef or wall that most divers are unaware that there is a vast ocean beyond their tiny piece of the reef. It is much more common to look reefward and find sea horses, frogfish, tiger groupers, queen angelfish, moray eels, etc. This makes Bonaire an exceptionally good place for fish photography and an ideal one for macro photography. It's also one of the best places in the Caribbean to take a photo course whether you're a beginner or ready for more advanced photo techniques.

No matter how many times you visit Bonaire, there always seems to be something new to see. The divemasters will let you know what and where the latest underwater show is taking place.

But don't miss the sights topside either. This is a picturesque island with spectacular photo opportunities from historic ruins to nature at its best to colorful island-style Dutch architecture.

Surface Intervals: For shopping and dining, Kralendijk; for photo ops, the Slave Huts at Washington Park, Willemstoren Lighthouse, the Salt Pier and, of course, the famous pink flamingoes. For some local color, Lac Bay fishing settlement at Cai (great windsurfing at Lac Bay!), Village of Rincon and Caves and Indian paintings at Playa Chiquito.

During the spring and summer months, schools of bigeye scads (Selar crumenophthalmus) swarm over the reefs along the west coast of Bonaire. (Photo: J. Schnabel)

Porpoises often swim close to shore along the coast of Klein Bonaire, sometimes sharing special moments with divers thrilled at their sight. (Photo: J. Schnabel)

A diver feels small swimming among the huge formations of mountainous star coral (Montastraea annularis) *at Playa Benge. (Photo: J. Schnabel)* ▶

Bonaire is a good choice for a vacation if you have children in tow. Several resorts have children's program not only designed to give you time to relax but to educate your children about the ocean and even teach them how to snorkel.

5

Cayman Islands

Its cloudless sapphire skies, diamond white beaches, and aquamarine waters belie a legendary history of treasures, and pirates with notorious names like Blackbeard and Long John Silver. The Cayman Islands are no longer under the control of swashbuckling buccaneers, and the treasures you'll discover on these islands are natural ones—spectacular walls, lush coral gardens, and fish-filled wrecks. Among divers around the world, these are equally legendary.

The Cayman Islands are part of the Cayman Ridge that descends more than a mile to the seafloor. They are the only three points at which the summits of this submerged mountain range break the surface. Just south of the islands, ocean depths reach more than 24,000 feet in the deepest known trench in Caribbean.

Not only do thousands of divers take their first dive vacation in Cayman, but tens of thousands of divers return to take another taste of world class diving in a world class destination. According to the Cayman government, 25% of the 250,000 tourists who visit the Cayman Islands each year are divers, making it one of the five most visited diving destinations in the world. And indeed, divers do make the pilgrimage to the islands from near and far.

The reasons range from the quality, size, and diversity of the accessible underwater environment to the watersports industry's reputation for excellence and safety to the rare opportunity for close encounters with spectacular marine life.

But for most divers, it is the offshore walls that plunge from the lip of the shallow reef to the 5,000-foot-deep ocean bottom that bring them back year after year. And while it may sound dramatic and adventurous, the diving conditions guarantee maximum enjoyment. With water temperatures averaging 80°F topside and underwater, little or no current, no island run-off so the visibility is consistently good, and calm boat rides, it's hard to beat. In addition, because your deep wall diving is limited by your bottom time or your experience, there are plenty of shallower walls, reefs, wrecks and even shore dives to keep you busy. And, of course, there are the close encounters with kissing stingrays, glimmering tarpon and a dancing manta.

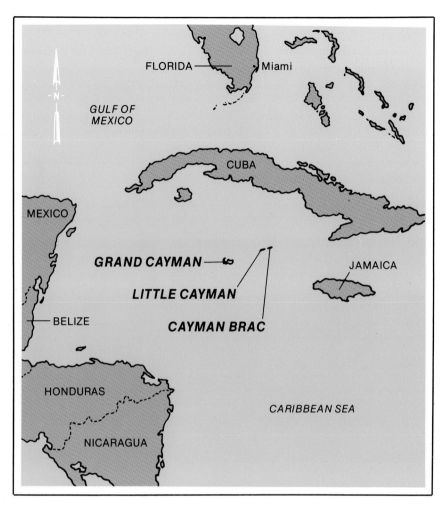

The Cayman Islands are located in the center of the Caribbean Sea along the edge of the 24,000-foot-deep (10 kilometers) Cayman Trench.

While the walls made Cayman famous among divers, the stingrays catapulted it into worldwide notoriety. **Stingray City** is unquestionably one of the greatest 12-foot dives for divers or snorkelers. It has been talked about, written about, and probably visited more than any other dive site in the world. Where else can you pet a dozen stingrays and have them pet you back!

But Stingray City is only one of many dives that have earned the Grand Cayman its reputation. **The Walls** in Cayman are unsurpassed in steepness, depth and coral coverage. And there are also beautiful shallow reefs which offer underwater photographers some of the best photo ops and maximal bottom time.

Cool dives:
- North Side: Grand Canyon, Hepp's Pipeline, Stingray City, North Sound Anchorage, New Tarpon Alley, Eagle Ray Alley, Pete's Ravine, No-Name Reef, Bringley's Bay.
- West Side: Balboa Wreck, The Aquarium, Peter's Reef, Victoria House Reef, Oro Verde Wreck , Royal Palms Reef, Soto's Reef, Devil's Grotto, Eden Rocks, Bonnie's Arch , Paul's Reef, Trinity Caves, Orange Canyon, The Tunnel, Pinnacle Rock, Lambert's Cave.
- East Side: Julie's Wall, The Maze, Snapper Hole.
- South Side: Original Tarpon Alley, South Sound Garden, South Sound Drop-off, Red Bay Gardens.

Welcome to the Cayman Islands! Keep a sharp eye because some of the most fascinating things, such as this frogfish, come in small packages. (Photo: C. Roessler)

A diamond blenny hides among the tentacles of a large anemone. The anemone subdues prey by stinging them with its waving tentacles. For small fish such as the blenny, which are immune to the toxin, the tentacles are a perfect refuge. (Photo: C. Roessler)

Hot Sightings: Sheer walls plunging out of sight, tunnels, caverns, arches, dense sponges, antler coral, basket sponges, gorgonians, sea whips, staghorn coral, lobsters, blue tangs, snappers, groupers, tame stingrays, tarpons, spotted trunkfish, bluestriped grunts, goatfish, porgy, wrasses, parrotfish, horse-eye jacks, sea breams, jewfish, eels, barracudas, basket sponges, trumpetfish, hogfish, French angels, eagle rays, and orange elephant ear sponges.

Super Snorkels: Balboa Wreck, Devil's Grotto.

In the past, **Little Cayman** and **Cayman Brac** have attracted the more seasoned divers who were more than willing to forgo sunbathing, ritzy resorts and nightclubs for world-class walls. Little by little, less experienced divers discovered that they too could enjoy the sheer spectacles of walls that start quite shallow and can be accessed by boat or from shore.

Little Cayman, of course, is synonymous with **Bloody Bay Wall.** It is a legendary place among divers who frequent the Caribbean, and it is an area visited by Cayman Brac dive operators as well. Along with **Jackson Bay,** there are few wall diving areas that are better. More than 20 moorings mark dive sites along where divers reach the drop-off at 20 feet in some spots, only to be confronted by unimaginably colorful and diverse sponges and corals that blanket the vertical precipice.

To cap what is already an unforgettable dive experience, Molly, Little Cayman's resident 10-foot manta ray, regularly cruises by or joins night dives to feed on the plankton attracted by divers lights.

Eagle Ray Alley, a gash in the face of the North Wall almost 30 feet (10 meters) deep, was named for the huge rays that are seen cruising the wall here. (Photo: C. Roessler) ▶

Molly the Manta

Have you ever wondered why a manta ray somersaults over and over again? This is the way giant mantas like Little Cayman's Molly feed. Manta rays are seen most often in waters clouded with plankton, on which they feed. The greener and more plankton-filled the water, the more likely you are to see a manta. In Little Cayman, dive masters discovered that by shining their lights in the water at night, they attracted plankton to the lights even though by day the surrounding waters are quite clear. As the plankton swarmed around the night lights, the island's resident manta ray appeared to feast on her favorite delicacy. On cue, Molly begins her elegant and perfectly choreographed somersaulting dance that enables her to scoop in the minuscule nutrients through her expansive mouth.

Manta rays like Molly can have a wing span of 10 feet across or more. Each manta ray has a distinctive marking or pattern on its underside and no two patterns are alike, so they can be distinguished from one another. And even if you can't tell one from another, there's no more breathtaking vision than watching one of these spectacular winged creatures glide effortlessly through the water.

The deep precipices of Cayman's walls draw divers like a magnet. In these clear calm waters, it's easy to forget how deep you really are. While diving Cayman, listen carefully to the information on each dive site given by the divemasters. Carefully monitor your depth gauge, watch, and pressure gauge during each dive. (Photo: C. Roessler)

Sting Ray City offers a unique opportunity for divers to get a very close view of some very interesting creatures. (Photo: C. Roessler) ▶

Eagle Rays, so called because of their size and the majestic sweep of their wings, are commonly seen as they move in to feed on crustaceans on the sandy bottom of North Sound. (Photo: C. Roessler)

This huge black grouper was found at Lambert's Cove. Although they ordinarily stay in deep water, the curious fish will sometimes ascend to within the depth range of sport divers. When annoyed, the groupers "boom" loudly, making a sound like a huge bass drum to frighten intruders. (Photo: C. Roessler)

Cool Dives in Little Cayman and Cayman Brac: Jackson Point, Bloody Bay Wall, Western Bloody Bay Wall, Anchor Wall, Charlie's Reef, Inside Out, Radar Reef, Tarpon Reef, East Chute.

One feature that brings divers to Cayman repeatedly is the quantity and diversity of the diving. It never becomes tiresome because there is so much of it. The official Cayman Islands diving guide lists 119 named sites in Grand Cayman, 37 in Cayman Brac and 41 in Little Cayman, approximately 30 professional dive operators, and over 70 dive boats. But numbers don't tell the entire story. Cayman's dive industry truly has its act together in terms of superb organization and operation. It is a dive destination that not only promotes its diving aggressively, but follows up by catering to divers' specific and diverse needs.

For new divers or divers coming to Cayman for a resort or certification course, Cayman also ranks at the top, not only because the weather and water conditions are "gentle," but because the dive operators are among the most safety conscious in the Caribbean.

The walls of the island are an open invitation to engage in deep decompression dives. Unless you have been trained in deep diving techniques, resist the temptation to go beyond the no-decompression limits. Hanging on an anchor line, waiting for the nitrogen to subside before surfacing, is not a practice for novices. (Photo: C. Roessler)

Surface Intervals: Great duty-free shopping and plenty of it, restaurants galore, active night life, Seven Mile Beach, the Turtle Farm, Atlantis Sub (especially for snorkelers), and historic George Town with its natural history museums.

The Cayman Islands are known as much for their offshore banking industry and beaches as for diving, so you'll notice a lot of mainstream tourists who have never even considered donning a scuba tank. But they know a good thing when they see it—with the highest standard of living in the Caribbean, these islands are pretty, well-maintained and very, very safe.

53

6

Cozumel

Twelve miles from the east coast of Mexico's Yucatan Peninsula lies the island of Cozumel. It is a relaxing getaway where the mysteries of an ancient civilization blend gently with the pleasures of a tropical resort, and where the clearest waters and most spectacular reefs have made it one of the finest watersports destinations in the world.

To the Maya, Cozumel was a sacred shrine. Mayan women would make the 12-mile pilgrimage by boat to worship Ix-Chel (the goddess of fertility and the wife of Itzamna, the supreme lord and sun god) at least once during their lifetime. Today, divers worship the fertile sea around Cozumel, and it is truly an underwater Mecca to which every diver should make a pilgrimage at least once. Many become so enchanted with this Mexican paradise that they return again and again.

According to a recent survey conducted by a major dive magazine, dives chose Cozumel as the most popular single island in the world. That is not so surprising if you consider what Cozumel has to offer beneath the surface.

The currents of the Yucatan flow between Cozumel and the mainland keeping the water clean and clear and, simultaneously carrying nourishing nutrients with it. With no rivers on either side of the channel and therefore no run-off, it isn't unusual to find 150 to 250 feet of visibility. In addition, because all the diving takes place along Cozumel's protected west coast on the lee side of the island, calm seas are the rule rather than the exception.

Cozumel ranks as Mexico's largest Caribbean island, running 12 miles along the Yucatan Peninsula. While there is approximately 25 miles of reef and walls, most of the diving action can be found on the reefs and diverse coral formations along the west coast that stretch from San Miguel to the southern end of the island.

Shallower areas close to shore offer some excellent opportunities for snorkelers to explore the marine life around the patch reefs, mini ledges and small coral heads. Easy diving in 40–60 foot depths offers higher profile coral heads and larger fish. The real excitement comes, however, on

A varied selection of large and small oceanfront resorts provides visitors to Cozumel with accommodations for every lifestyle and budget. (Photo: S. Cummings) ▶

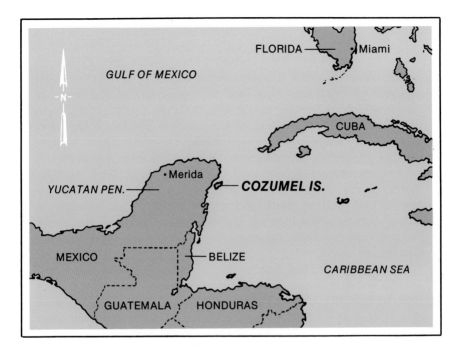

Nestled under the protection arm of Mexico's Yucatan peninsula, Cozumel provides some of the most spectacular diving in the hemisphere.

Drift Diving

The Caribbean has a reputation among divers and snorkelers for the calmest, clearest waters in the world. At some dive sites, however, you can add "currents" to the list of C's. The currents do not affect the surface conditions, but they can affect the style of diving in that area. When dive operators determine that drift diving is the most effective and efficient way for divers to deal with the prevailing currents, you are in for the ride of your life!

Currents bring nutrients and clear water with them as they sweep past the reefs and walls, so many current dives can be spectacular. But, as seasoned divers know, as exhilarating as diving with a current may be, trying to swim against it back to a moored dive boat can expend a lot of air and energy. The solution is drift diving.

On drift dives, dive boats do not anchor on the reefs and wrecks—in fact, often there are no moorings—and divers don't have to fight the current to return to a stationary boat. Different dive operators in different destinations may have slightly different styles for drift diving. In some places, dive masters will carry a tag line with a surface float that marks the group's location underwater. In others, two dive masters guide the divers along the reef or wall so the group surfaces at the same time. Others are simply excellent bubble watchers and can estimate the location of the divers by observing divers' bubbles as they reach the surface, as long as the water is clear and calm.

When divers complete their drift dive, the dive boat picks them up wherever they surface. It does not take much to get the "drift" of diving with the currents!

the deeper reefs where the huge coral formations tantalize divers with a plethora of dramatic undercuts, swimthroughs, and caverns that provide a backdrop for elegant gorgonians and vibrantly hued sponges.

Divers and snorkelers of all levels will enjoy a visit to Cozumel's most popular reef, **Palancar.** At this national underwater park, you will come upon stunning plateaus, canyons, and walls in as little as 25 feet.

Another aspect of diving in Cozumel that makes it both unique and particularly appealing to seasoned divers is the drift diving. In fact, because there are no moorings around the island and there is almost always a current, especially on the deeper dives, most dives are done as drift dives.

The visibility along Cozumel's reefs often ranges from 150–200 feet, so you'll almost always get a very clear view of all the wonders that this most popular of dive destinations has to offer. (Photo: S. Cummings) ▶

And if you've never done a drift dive before, Cozumel has an unbelievable treat in store for you. Imagine freefalling horizontally, cruising comfortably along a reef without expending any energy to move yourself forward, and never having to kick against a current to get back to the dive boat! That's Cozumel diving!

Because drift diving is so common, and dive boats don't have moored sites to identify specific locations, dive sites refer to a "vicinity." About 40 sites have names and general locations used by all the local dive operators.

Cozumel also differs from many of the Caribbean dive destinations in that an overwhelming number of the local dive operators operate independently of the hotels. So, it is not unusual to dive with an operator located in town or at a different hotel or even to dive with several different operators during your vacation. If your hotel does not have a dive operation on premises, most dive boats will arrange to pick you up at your hotel dock for your convenience.

Hard corals and sponges decorate a natural archway at Tormentos. (Photo: S. Cummings)

San Miguel, Cozumel's main street, is lined with hundreds of bustling shops and restaurants, and night clubs. (Photo: S. Cummings)

There are abundant opportunities to enjoy the wonderful food and beverages of Cozumel's many resturants, but don't let overindulgence ruin your or your buddy's diving fun. (Photo: S. Cummings)

Heading out for that first dive of the day—no matter whether it's Palancar, Santa Rosa, or any of Cozumel's other jewels—is always a time for excited anticipation and proper preparation. (Photo: S. Cummings)

◄ *Cozumel's currents provide a preponderance of drift diving that allows you to "fly" over spectacular coral heads crowned with dazzling arrays of sponges and gorgonians. (Photo: S. Cummings)*

Cool Dives: Paraiso Reef North, Airplane Flats, Paraiso Reef South, Chankanab, Beachcomber Cavern, Tormentos, Yocab, El Paso del Cedral, Tunich, Cardona, San Francisco, Santa Rosa, Palancar, Punta Sur, Colombia Reef, Maracaibo, Colombia Shallows.

Hot Sightings: Large approachable groupers, coral toadfish, octopus, green and spotted moray eels, caves and grottos, plate corals, sponges, large pelagics.

Super Snorkels: Airplane Flats, Paraiso Reef South, Chankanab (lagoon), Columbia Shallows

Surface Intervals: One thing all visitors agree on is that surface intervals in Cozumel are never dull. It is an island where entertainment is non-stop, authentic margaritas and fajitas hot off the grill are the order of the day, and a festive Mexican flamboyance flavors every activity. There are more than 100 good restaurants not to mention night clubs, lounges, and discos, more than 200 gift shops, every watersport you can imagine, hotel theme nights, sports tournaments and festivals, and tour services that will whisk you away to discover the wonders of the ancient Mayan civilization on the Yucatan Peninsula. Cozumel even has its own Museum and Archeological Park.

7

Dominica

There are only a handful of islands left in the Caribbean that have not undergone the heavy hand of over-zealous developers. Dominica is among the few. It is the kind of island that reminds us of what the Caribbean used to be—sleepy, quiet, pristine—or, if we did not experience the Caribbean of 20 or 30 years ago, undeveloped and unspoiled by too many tourists and cruise ships, it makes us yearn for the days before condos, time shares, and mega-resorts.

Ten years ago, few had heard of Dominica—which isn't to say it is now a household name. But eco-tourism had not yet been coined, there were no posters hanging in travel agents' offices, and its distinctive underwater environment had not yet caught the attention of divers. Slowly, this precious hideaway with its rare combination of natural treasures topside and underwater, its colorful pure West Indian ambiance, and its warm, welcoming islanders, is gaining exposure as a unique and premiere eco-tourist destination, not only among naturalists, but divers as well.

What strikes visitors first is the raw physical beauty of Dominica. Morne Diablotin, the largest mountain on Dominica, looms over the island topping out at an altitude of 4,747 feet above sea level, higher than any other island in the eastern Caribbean. Like Saba, another island of volcanic origin, Dominica is a breathtaking blend of sheer precipitous cliffs and softly sloping valleys veiled in variegated shades of green.

While many islands have succumbed to the tourist penchant for discos and steel bands, Dominican music is a symphony of sound—of birds singing, raindrops falling against leaves, waterfalls rushing down cliffs. Whether you visit Dominica as an avid and enthusiastic eco-tourist or not, you will be converted during your stay because here nature surrounds and envelops you unlike anywhere else in the Caribbean.

Tropical rain forests, cascading waterfalls, and a 100-foot-high canopy of jungle trees that cloak a virtual botanical museum of unusual flora are just a few of Dominica's specialties. Natural hot springs and the second largest "boiling lake" in the world are fueled by the lava that still bubbles below the island's surface. Outdoor and nature photographers will be in paradise in Dominica.

"The Father" is one of the dramatic twin falls at Dominica's famous Trafalgar Falls, a popular tourist attraction. (Photo: M. Lawrence) ▶

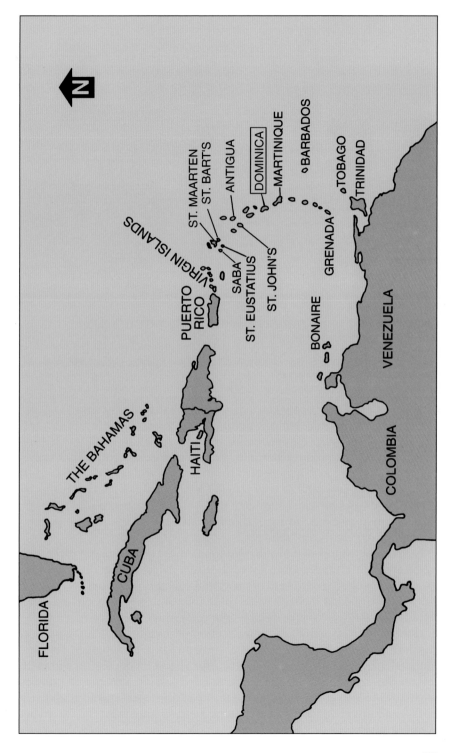

Fishing boats add a colorful touch to the beach at Souffriere Bay in Dominica. (Photo: M. Lawrence)

A diver swims among the golden crinoids and tube sponges at Dangleben's Pinnacles in Dominica. (Photo: M. Lawrence) ▶

Many of the Caribbean islands that boast great visibility tend to be arid flat landfalls with little annual rain to blur their waters with silty run-off. But Dominica's moist climate belies this theory. Along with the arching rainbows and cascading waterfalls that have become Dominica's trademark, the marine environment also benefits from the rainfall in this case. What sediment does find its way into the water attracts hungry chromis by the hundreds and provides nutrients that nourish the corals and sponges, and contribute not only to the healthiness of the reef life but the surprising size of the corals and sponges.

Despite the abundance of rain Dominica experiences, underwater visibility constantly ranges from 60 to 100 feet. Most of the dive sites are located along the leeward side of the island which is drier, and because the island is surrounded by deep water close to shore, any sediment that does run off into the water sinks quickly and disappears from divers' view.

Dominica offers a fine, diverse selection of dive sites all along its west coast. Dive sites feature such unusual formations as a submerged volcano, multitudes of coral encrusted pinnacles that rise from the reef to within 20 feet of the surface, underwater fumeroles releasing streams of bubbles into the water, caves and caverns, open ocean dive sites, and an abundance of fish and invertebrate life everywhere. With so much variety, the diving is never repetitious or uneventful.

Dominica is one of the very few undeveloped remnants of how Caribbean islands used to be 30 years ago, so visit this diamond in the rough before it's discovered. (Photo: S. Cummings)

◄ *Anemones, sponges, and arrow crabs create a symphony of color and movement at Scott's Head Pinnacles in Dominica. (Photo: M. Lawrence)*

Cool Dives: Soufriere Pinnacles, La Bim Wall, Bangleben's Reef, Dangleben's Pinnacles, Scott's Head Drop-off and Scott's Head Pinnacles, Condo, Village and Suburbs, Champagne, Point Guignard, Maggie's Point, Coral Gardens North, Whale Shark Reef, Nose Reef, Barry's Dream, Douglas Point Drop-off, Toucari Bay.

Hot Sightings: Pinnacles, fumeroles, caves, finger coral, barrel sponges, crinoids, black coral trees, frogfish, sea horses, flying gunards, batfish, nudibranchs, ocean pelagics, schooling blackbar soldierfish, glassy sweepers, dense schools of fish.

Surface Intervals: A leisurely walk to Emerald Pool through the woods to a grotto at edge of the rain forest, a full day hike for hearty explorers to Dominica's highest peak, Morne Diablotin, a visit to one or more of the island's spectacular waterfalls—Middleham, Sari-Sari, Victoria Falls, or Trafalgar Falls whose two falls, the Father and the Mother, are the most photogenic; a relaxing spa bath at the hot spring at the mouth of Titou Gorge, or a serious two- to three-hour hike to Boiling Lake.

Dominica is perhaps the most unusual and rustic of the Caribbean dive destinations. It is truly a naturalist's haven and for divers who desire someplace unexploited and undiscovered, it is the ultimate paradise.

8

Saba

Saba is one of five islands spread throughout the Caribbean that comprise the Netherland Antilles. Do not be surprised if you have not heard of it. It is not exactly a bastion of tourism much to its advantage. But if mountains and huge pinnacles—above and below the sea—excite you, Saba is a rare find in the Caribbean.

Those who have the distinct pleasure of visiting Saba leave it with a very special feeling. A sense they have discovered a secret, a breathtaking sanctuary somehow protected from the fast and often careless pace of the modern world.

There are not many places like Saba left in the Caribbean and it is not the classic Caribbean island with long white sand beaches and big fancy resorts. Instead it is a strikingly dramatic volcanic rock that rises 3,000 feet above the sea from steep cliffs rather than beaches.

Saba is a world of its own. Its charm never seems to diminish with the years. It is one of the most captivating islands in the Caribbean. It's the kind of place you'd go to write your novel.

The island is accessible by boat or plane via St. Maarten and either way you arrive, the approach is nothing less than spectacular. Even from a distance as you approach by boat, an atmosphere of mystery seems to surround it much as the clouds that envelop the top of its looming mountain. By air it can be quite exciting as you land on a small runway carved out of the rocky shoreline!

Actually, Saba is a very small island, only about 5 square miles with a population of around 1,100. As we all know, great things come in small packages and Saba is no exception.

To describe Saba as picturesque is to understate the fact. From the cloud-draped summit of Mt. Scenery with its rain forests to the charming white, green, and red cottages that dot the mountainsides and cluster in small villages at towns with names like the Bottom and Windwardside, Saba is a photographer's dream come true.

A rock island covered by lush greenery and capped by the "Elfin Forest," a mountaintop rain forest of mountain mahogany trees and over 60 species of birds, it is a place of refuge and fascination for naturalists unlike anything you'll see anywhere else in the Caribbean.

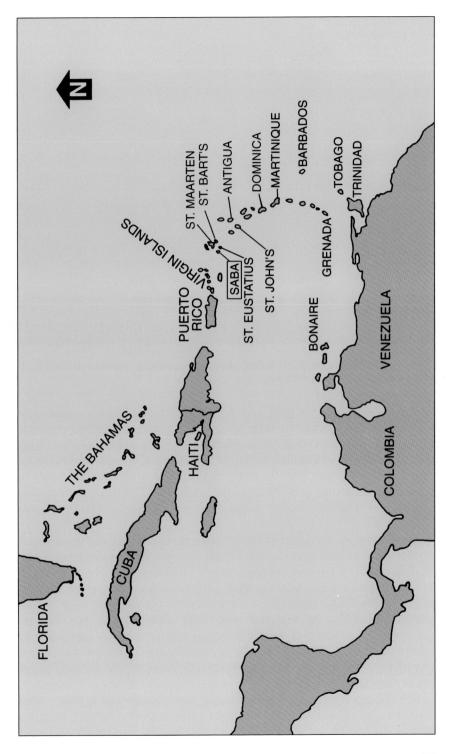

N

FLORIDA

THE BAHAMAS

CUBA

HAITI

PUERTO RICO

VIRGIN ISLANDS

ST. MAARTEN

ST. BART'S

SABA

ST. EUSTATIUS

ST. JOHN'S

ANTIGUA

DOMINICA

MARTINIQUE

BARBADOS

TOBAGO

TRINIDAD

GRENADA

BONAIRE

VENEZUELA

COLOMBIA

The summit of Mt. Scenery in Saba rises almost vertically to an elevation of 2,989 ft. above sea level. (Photo: J. Bourque)

The island locals are generous with historical anecdotes about their island. Most likely you will hear about it from your taxi driver who provides the best and most affordable way to tour the island. You will hear about "the road that couldn't be built" as he drives you up unimaginably steep stretches from "The Bottom" to Elfin Forest. It took 21 years to build the 9-mile road that Dutch engineers had told them was impossible to construct. That they built it themselves tells you a little about the Saban personality!

About 30 years ago, the road was complete, the airport was opened and the harbor was built and, for all intents and purposes, Saba entered the modern world. However, only to a point. The houses all over the island, new as well as old, still bear the trademark white paint with green shutters and red roofs. There is no crime; hitchhiking is not only safe here, it's an accepted tradition. Developers who have changed the face of the Caribbean have left this beautiful island untouched. Accommodations consist of 50 rooms in five hotels and guesthouses, cottages and villas. The biggest development the island has seen is the 40-room condo resort that is scheduled to open soon.

The Sabans welcome tourists warmly and proudly share their island paradise with visitors. But they also recognize that many of their precious natural resources such as the rain forest and the reefs are fragile and must

Photo Tips—Shooting Against Black Sand

If you're visiting volcanic islands like Saba and Dominica, beware of the "black sand"—but only if you're an underwater photographer. The black sand is a result of the lava that has been granulated with time and erosion, and creates a dark colored sand instead of the fine white and pink sand you'll find on most Caribbean islands. It won't affect the beauty of the dive environment to the naked eye, but it will drastically affect the quality of your photography unless you make adjustments to compensate.

The dark sand absorbs much more light than white sand. If you set your F-stop to your customary setting, your photos will be dark, much darker than you would have expected. The solution is to open up your F-stop by one to two stops, depending on how reflective your subject is and how dark the bottom is.

The best way to find out how much adjustment you need is to shoot a roll on your first dive and process it as soon as possible, so you can see the effect of the darker background. There is nothing more disappointing than arriving home after your vacation only to find that every shot was underexposed!

Saba director of tourism Glen Holm and photographer Susan Swygert study lava formations below Flat Point, Saba. (Photo: J. Schnabel)

be protected for future generations. Toward this goal, the Saba Conservation Foundation has the task of preserving and managing the island's natural resources topside and underwater.

Divers may not have been quick to discover Saba, but once they did, the dive tourism business on the island has grown steadily. Fortunately, the Saba government and dive operators had the foresight to protect the marine environment, and in 1987 they formally established the Saba Marine Park to preserve and manage Saba's marine resources. Similar to other marine parks around the Caribbean, the park at Saba includes the waters and seabed from the high-water mark to a depth of 200 feet, as well as two prominent offshore seamounts.

Saba is one of the most outspokenly eco-aware and eco-active dive destinations in the Caribbean. They make no bones about their commitment to preserving the reefs around the island, and they make sure every diver knows about it as well. They take an active role in educating divers about the reefs and what diver damage does to them. When you submerge on these dive sites, you will not only understand their vigilance, you will appreciate the result of their protective attitude and practices.

Thirty-three permanent dive site moorings now mark excellent marine habitats for divers to explore, all within about a 20-minute ride by boat from Saba's only harbor, Fort Bay Harbor.

Saba's reef system may well be one of the last truly pristine marine environments in the Caribbean. The conditions are ideal for healthy and sustained growth. With no runoff or pollutants to taint the surrounding waters and with deep water and its life-sustaining nutrients so close to shore, the marine environment thrives.

Human interaction with Saba's underwater world has been minimal. In fact, only about 4,000 divers a year visit the island's reefs, walls, and trademark pinnacles. With comparatively little impact on the fish habitats and eco-system, the waters are full of interesting aquatic life and the diving is highly varied from site to site.

The underwater scene with its volcanic pinnacles echoes the rugged terrain topside. But here, instead of towering trees and tropical vegetation of the rain forest with its fabulous array of bird life, hard corals have transformed underwater pinnacles and walls into a dense and richly hued forest for the resident marine creatures.

Cool Dives: Tent Reef, Tent Wall (night diving!!!), Third Encounter, Twilight Zone, Outer Limits, Diamond Rock, The Needle.

Hot Sightings: Huge undersea mountains and pinnacles, walls blanketed with brightly colored sponges and encrusting corals, large barrel sponges, tube sponges, patch reef, elkhorn coral forest, French angelfish, pelagics, garden eels, upwelling hot springs, creole wrasses, brown chromis, black durgeons, occasional black top sharks, orange elephant ear sponges, barracudas, groupers, jacks, turtles, sharks, and rays.

Lush greenery adorns the mountaintop at the Captain's Quarters hotel on Saba. (Photo: S. Swygert)

Surface Intervals: Sightseeing tour by taxi; shopping for locally made items, especially handmade batik prints, lace, and Saba Spice; stairway to walk up into the rain forest; and hiking seven marked nature trails. Pick up a Saba Nature Trails brochure at the tourist office on the island. For the adventurous, travel from St. Maarten to Saba by air. The only level spot on the island is the 1,312-foot-long runway at the airport surrounded on three sides by sheer cliffs that plunge into the sea and on the fourth side by a sheer cliff that soars upward toward the town of Hell's Gate! For the less hearty, a simple visit to the airport will suffice!

9

Turks & Caicos Islands

If you follow the Bahamas chain to the southernmost end and move your finger just a little farther south on the map, you will come to the tiny archipelago of the Turks and Caicos Islands. They may not be quite as "untouched" by the modern world as they were ten or fifteen years ago when divers first began to explore the fabulous diving there, but they really have not changed much. They still offer that uncrowded, off the beaten-track feel of islands that have not yet been "discovered" by the rest of the vacation-going world.

Only **Providenciales** has felt the influence of foreign developers and even here, full-scale resorts are few and far between and the small number of condos are upscale, tastefully designed, and intimate. As for the other islands, accommodations consist of a smattering of small, quaint beachfront hotels that make up in ambiance and charm what they lack in spit and shine. But it is not the island ambiance that accounts for the appeal Turks and Caicos has for divers—it is the excellent diving. And the dive operators in the Turks and Caicos, liveaboard and landbased alike, are as professional and knowledgeable as you will find anywhere.

A 50-mile-long barrier reef that runs along the northern side of the Turks and Caicos chain and protects the islands is what produces the underwater spectacle that has earned this destination its growing reputation as one of the Caribbean's best places to submerge. Situated between the Atlantic Ocean and the Caribbean, they are the perfect model of "sleepy little islands," with little to offer in the way of international retail shops, five-star restaurants and flashy discos. But as quiet and unobtrusive as they may be topside, the entertainment underwater deserves a top rating for its dramatic vertical walls, lush coral gardens, colorful tropical fish, and large pelagics including humpback whales that make frequent, albeit unannounced, appearances at the local dive sites.

The beauty of Turks and Caicos walls and lush coral reefs is enhanced by regular sightings of dolphins and humpback whales on the surface, and underwater encounters with turtles, eagle rays, or manta rays. The dry climate almost guarantees better than average visibility for the Caribbean ranging from 60–150 feet or more depending on the season and prevailing weather and tides.

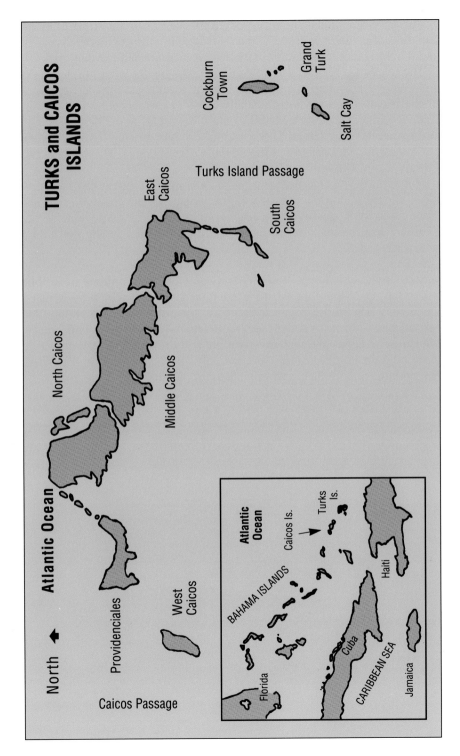

TURKS and CAICOS ISLANDS

North ◄ Atlantic Ocean

North Caicos

East Caicos

Cockburn Town

Grand Turk

Salt Cay

Turks Island Passage

South Caicos

Middle Caicos

Providenciales

West Caicos

Caicos Passage

Atlantic Ocean

BAHAMA ISLANDS

Caicos Is.

Turks Is.

Florida

Cuba

Haiti

CARIBBEAN SEA

Jamaica

75

The government and the dive operators make a valiant effort to maintain the quality and condition of the reefs with moorings at most dive sites and the designation of certain marine areas as protected national parks.

The renowned **Grand Turk** "wall" is undoubtedly what put the Turks and Caicos on the map as a dive destination. Running along the west coast of the island, the wall lies unusually close to the shoreline it parallels. Calm lee waters, excellent visibility, short boat rides to the dive sites, and shallow walls make Grand Turk nothing less than nirvana for avid divers.

Cool Dives: McDonald's, Amphitheatre, Black Forest, The Anchor, The Library, Coral Gardens, and Tunnels.

Hot Sightings: Large orange elephant ear sponges (great for photography), stingrays, turtles and sizable groupers, vibrant encrusting corals, black coral trees, passageways and swimthroughs, dramatic wall views, excellent invertebrate life on night dives, and whales during the winter migrating season.

Salt Cay may only be 7 miles from Grand Turk, but it might as well be a world away. Visiting the island is like taking a step back in time. Modern technology has brushed against Salt Cay, but just barely. Telephones and fax machines, electricity and flushing toilets have made their appearance, but kerosene lamps and water cisterns are still the order of the day. Traffic jams are unheard of because there are only one or two cars on the island, and nothing is more than a short walk away, including the dive boat.

Whale Watching

There is nothing quite as exciting as sighting whales in the distance. You never know where or when you might see them, but the telltale stream of mist on the horizon as they spout will alert the attentive whale watcher of their presence in the area. Throughout the Caribbean, sightings of pilot and humpbacks are fairly common (relative to other whales, although whale sightings are never common!) While it may seem that whales sightings are random, there are places they appear on a fairly regular basis. The Silver Banks off of the Dominican Republic and the Turks Passage in the Turks and Caicos Islands are among these.

During the winter months, humpback whales begin their annual migration southward. during which they give birth to their offspring. Once the mothers have "calved," they attend closely to the babies. It is the one time that you may actually be able to approach a whale on the surface within a relatively close range.

Normally, the mother will instinctively submerge into deeper water at any impending intrusion. However, because her natural instinct to protect her newborn, who cannot dive very deep, supersedes any reflex to avoid confrontation, she will remain on or near the surface.

Sometimes you may see only a single mother and baby and other times you will observe several traveling in a pod. Most likely, during whale migration season, if you see one, there are many more in the area so keep your eyes peeled to the horizon.

If you approach slowly and quietly, you may be lucky enough to watch these gentle giants pass within a few feet of your boat. It is a rare opportunity but an unforgettable experience to view these enormous and gentle mammals at close view. The local island residents and dive masters tend to know the best times and best places to whale watch. Liveaboard dive boats also set aside special trips that concentrate on whale watches, and their mobility enables them to cover a lot of ocean in their search.

If you are fortunate enough to be in the water with whales, be patient and let them come to you. In most places, it is illegal to approach or harass whales in any way and local governments take this very seriously. If you're diving in an area where whales have recently been sighted, listen closely. You might just hear a whale song somewhere off in the distance!

◄ The uninhabited island of West Caicos is known for its excellent wall diving and its pristine white beaches. (Photo: S. Cummings)

All of the dive sites in Grand Turk are accessible to divers staying in Salt Cay, but Salt Cay has a few of its own worthy of a visit.

Cool Dives: Point Pleasant, Northwest Wall, Kelly's Folly and Black Coral Canyon. This is a great place to explore new, undiscovered sites.

Hot Sightings: Expansive stands of elkhorn coral, dramatic pillar coral, walls covered with deep sea gorgonians, tube, barrel and twisted rope sponges, moray eels, and hawksbill turtles.

Like Grand Turk, the whales cruise by Salt Cay during the winter months, and dolphins and mantas are seen during the summertime.

Three dive areas are visited regularly from **Provo—West Caicos, Northwest Point** and **Grace Bay.** Each area offers a distinctly different dive experience and as to the question of which is the best, that depends on who you're asking.

West Caicos's 2-mile-long wall lies a mere quarter mile from the shore. It begins at about 45–60 feet and bottoms out somewhere around 6,000 feet with visibility 100 feet plus. No two dives are quite the same and several of them have unusually distinctive features.

Cool Dives: Land of the Giants, Midnite Manta, Highway to Heaven, Gully, Rock Garden Interlude, Elephant Ear Canyon, Driveway, Whiteface, Sunday Service, and Isle's End.

Hot Sightings: Black coral trees, deep water seafans, cleaning stations, hard corals and invertebrates, multi-colored sponge-studded walls, a 10-foot-by-10-foot orange elephant ear sponge not to be missed, schooling fish, and an occasional shark, manta ray or eagle ray.

Surface Interval: If time permits it, take a walk on this uninhabited island where the remnants of an old salt raking industry are still evident and nature has found a friendly sanctuary.

The sites at **Northwest Point** are located along 3 miles of vertical wall. The dramatic coral formation of the wall is heavily sculpted by ravines, holes, caves, swimthroughs, arches, and seamounts, which provide interesting surfaces for healthy marine growth to flourish.

Cool Dives: Hole in the Wall, The Stairway, Black Coral Forest, Canyons, The Crack, Shark Hotel, Amphitheatre, and Mystery Reef.

Hot Sightings: All the nooks and crannies that invite exploration, a towering pinnacle that makes a dramatic wide-angle subject, schooling fish on the reefs, sharks, oversized orange elephant ear sponges, tall stands of pillar coral, lots of colorful sponges and tropical fish.

Closer to the resorts on the north shore are the dive sites along the spur and groove systems in **Grace Bay,** which feature excellent soft corals and gorgonians, especially below 50 feet where the wave activity has less effect. With dives beginning as shallow as 30 feet and bottoming out between 60–160 feet, it is ideal for novice through advance divers.

Cool Dives: The Pinnacles, The Closet, Grouper Hole, Shark Hole, and the wrecks, *Southwind* and *We.*

Hot Sightings: Black coral trees, friendly groupers, nurse sharks, wrecks.

The beach at Northwest Point in Provo, only accessible by boat or four-wheel drive vehicles, offers some interesting snorkeling including an occasional school of squid. (Photo: S. Cummings)

Certainly, the Turks and Caicos is not for everyone. It is not for those who must have a shopping fix at least once a day or are looking for a hot night life. But if superior diving and evenings swapping dive stories with fellow aquanauts is enough to make a vacation perfect, this is nirvana.

Surface Intervals: The uncrowded beaches. Grand Turk's Turks and Caicos National Museum, which houses the remains of a wooden sailing ship that lay undiscovered in 20 feet of water near West Caicos for 460 years. The vestiges of the salt raking industry on Salt Cay, a UNESCO World Heritage site. The Island Sea Center on Provo and its queen conch mariculture project, Jojo, the local bottlenosed dolphin, and Into the Blue, a dolphin rescue, rehabilitation and release program.

10

In and Around the Caribbean

The destinations described in this guide represent areas where the diving is recognized world wide for overall excellence and also offer some distinctive features that make them unique. This selection, however, is not intended to imply that there are not many other dive destinations around the Caribbean that offer very good and varied diving and promise a great overall dive vacation.

The United States Virgin Islands (St. Thomas, St. John, and St. Croix). These islands are U.S. territories and offer all the comforts and conveniences of home with the added flair of Caribbean style. Superb restaurants, night clubs, and a wide variety of hotels and resorts are available on all three islands, yet each island offers a distinctive ambiance of its own. St. Thomas is bustling and busy, St. John is quiet with a national park on more than three-quarters of the island, and St. Croix still retains a laid back island pace. All provide professional, full-service dive operations and diverse diving opportunities including wrecks, mini-walls and reefs. Don't miss Buck Island National Marine Park or the Fredericksted Pier at night.

British Virgin Islands. Still quite colonial in flavor, the BVI's are still known as a sailing paradise with picturesque marinas and an "off the beaten track" ambiance. The islands haven't been over-developed and the islanders are friendly. Underwater, the *Rhone* (Peter Benchley's *The Deep*) and the *Chiquizen* may well top the "Best Wreck Dives in the Caribbean" list.

Aruba and Curaçao. For topside activity, few places match these Netherland Antillean isles. With their strikingly colorful Dutch architecture, world class hotels, fabulous beaches, casinos and more restaurants than any one visitor could sample in a year, and world renowned windsurfing conditions, these destinations are worthy of a trip even if you never put a regulator in your mouth. However, if diving is on the agenda, they won't disappoint. Snorkelers as well as divers should make a point of visiting the wreck of the *Antilla* in Aruba. Sunk during World War II in shallow water, it's showing every bit of its age—in full color and overgrown glory!

Exploring the wonders of the Caribbean would take several lifetimes of diving—so you better hurry! (Photo: S. Cummings) ▶

11

Smart, Safe Diving

Preparation. Before you leave home, make sure all of your dive gear is in good working order and that all items that must be serviced yearly—especially regulators—have been. There is nothing as aggravating as getting on the boat and arriving on your first dive site, only to discover that your octopus is free-flowing. If you wear a mask with a prescription or have trouble finding a mask that fits you correctly, bring a backup mask. Masks have been known to arrive at a different destination than you, fall overboard, or break. You won't be comfortable with a borrowed mask if you can't see or if it keeps leaking. Finally, if you haven't been diving for 6 months or more, especially if you have logged fewer than 20 dives, it might be a good idea to take a practice or refresher dive either in a local pool at home or with an instructor at a dive store in Florida before you head for deep water.

Reef Etiquette and Buoyancy Control

While moorings may go a long way toward reducing anchor damage to our reefs, so far there is nothing to protect them from damage by divers, except divers. Dive sites tend to be located where the reefs and walls display the most beautiful corals and sponges. And it only takes a moment—an inadvertently placed hand or knee on the coral or an unaware brush or kick with a fin—to destroy this fragile living part of our delicate ecosystem. Only a moment to make a dive site a little less spectacular for other divers. Luckily, it only takes a little extra preparation and consideration to preserve it for generations of divers to come.

So, if you're a new diver, a little rusty after a long hiatus on dry land, diving with new equipment, or if you just haven't paid much attention to your reef etiquette or buoyancy control in the past, here are a few helpful tips how you can personally help preserve our underwater environment:

Weight Yourself Properly. Never dive with too much weight. (Northern divers—this means you! When you put on a lighter wetsuit or dive skin, shed some of those lead pounds, too!) Weight yourself so that you *float at eye level* on the surface with your lungs full of air and none in your BCD. Exhale fully and you should begin to sink. As your week of diving goes by and you relax underwater, drop some more weight. Ask your dive-master what kind of tank you're using. Tanks vary in their buoyancy when they are empty. You want to be able to hover comfortably at 15 feet to make your safety stop when your tank is low at the end of your dive.

Control Your Buoyancy with Your Breathing. If you are properly weighted and have successfully attained neutral buoyancy with your BCD at depth, you should be able to fine-tune your hovering capacity by inhaling and exhaling. Being able to rise and sink at will is the real trick to being able to hover and glide over and around the reef formations with grace and skill.

Avoid Fin Damage to Coral. Never stand (or kneel) on the corals. If you're hovering above the reef, keep your fins up off the reef. If you're swimming, do so in a horizontal position looking down so you're not flutter-kicking the reef. When you're easing through a narrow space such as a tunnel or gully between coral heads, keep an eye on where your feet are and, if necessary, make your kicks small and efficient to move you through the compact area. Reef etiquette also demands that, if you are swimming near a sandy bottom, stay several feet above the sand so you don't kick up any silt and ruin the dive for other divers.

Don't Touch the Reef. No matter how pretty and tactile the coral and sponges are, look but don't touch. And never, never grab onto the reef to steady yourself. If you need to stabilize yourself or keep from bumping into things or other divers, try using one or two fingers instead of your entire hand. And look for dead spots, areas between the corals or even the underside of a coral cranny where there is generally less growth. If, by chance, you see any trash on the reef, bring it up with you. If we all do our part, it will make a difference.

Fire coral may look like dead coral, but it packs a sensational sting if touched. (Photo: S. Cummings)

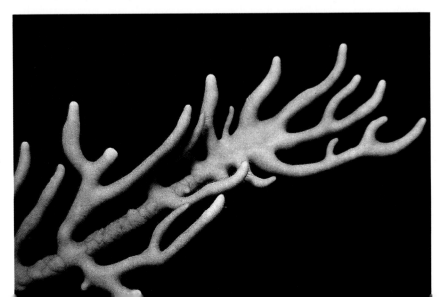

Watch Where You Land. If you need to touch down or kneel on solid ground, look for a sandy area in between the coral heads. If you need to take a photo, float or glide over your subject or steady yourself with a finger, but keep the rest of your body away from the reef. If you can't get the picture or see your subject without lying on the coral, don't take the picture!

Don't Drag Loose Gauges or Octopus Across the Reef. Hanging consoles, goody bags, tools, and other unsecured equipment can do as much damage to the corals as your hands and feet. Keep your equipment close to your body by tucking it into your BCD pockets or using retainer clips.

Don't Grab the Marine Creatures. Don't ride the turtles, grab the lobsters, chase the stingrays, or harass the eels. They are curious by nature and will gradually move toward you or stay still if you leave them alone. If you grab them, they'll disappear faster than you can clear your mask, and no one else will have a chance to see them either.

Be considerate. Leave the reef in the same condition in which you find it. In this way, it will remain healthy and thriving for future divers to enjoy.

Hazardous Marine Life

Diving in the Caribbean isn't really hazardous. It's divers who are hazardous. When was the last time a stand of fire coral pursued a diver to sting him? Most stings, scrapes, and punctures are due to divers inadvertently bumping into coral or touching a creature that instinctively defends itself against its giant aggressor. Some are harmless and merely uncomfortable. Others may require medical attention. Ideally, we shouldn't be touching anything underwater, but it does happen and it does hurt!

Watch out for the following:

Fire Coral. Mustard brown in color, fire coral is most often found in shallower waters encrusting dead gorgonians or coral. You may find it on the wrecks. Contact causes a burning sensation that lasts for several minutes and sometimes causes red welts on the skin. If you rub against fire coral, do not try to rub the affected area as you will spread the small stinging particles. Upon resurfacing, apply meat tenderizer to relieve the sting and then antibiotic cream. Cortisone cream can also reduce any inflammation.

Sponges. They may be beautiful, but sponges can also pack a powerful punch with fine spicules that sting on contact. While bright reddish brown ones are often the stinging kind, familiarly called "dread red," they are not the only culprits. If you touch a stinging sponge, scrape the area with the edge of your dive knife. Home remedies include mild vinegar or ammonia solutions to ease the pain, but if it will not subside within a day, again, cortisone cream might help.

Sea Urchins. The urchin's most dangerous weapon is its spines, which can penetrate neoprene wetsuits, booties, and gloves with ease. You'll know from the instant pain you've been jabbed. Urchins tend to be more common in shallow areas near shore and come out of their shelters under coral heads at night. If you are beach diving, beware of urchins that may be lying on the shallow reef you have to cross to reach deeper water. Don't move across it on your hands and knees; start swimming as soon as possible. Injuries should be attended to as soon as possible because infection can occur. Minor punctures require removal of the spine and treatment with an antibiotic cream. More serious ones should be looked at by a doctor.

Bristle Worms. These creatures make a great subject for macro photography but don't touch them to move them to the perfect spot. Use a strobe arm or dive knife. Contact will result in tiny stinging bristles being embedded in the skin and a burning feeling or welt. You can try to scrape the bristles off with the edge of a dive knife. Otherwise, they will work themselves out within a few days. Again, cortisone cream can help minimize any inflammation.

These six-foot purple tube sponges photographed at Rock Garden Interlude have graced the pages of several dive magazines. (Photo: S. Cummings)

Sea Wasps. A potentially serious diving hazard, sea wasps are small, potent jellyfish with four stinging tentacles, and they generally swim within a few feet of the surface at night. If sea wasps have been spotted in the water where you are planning to do a night dive, take caution. Don't linger on the surface upon entry into the water. When you return, turn your dive light off as it attracts them, and exit the water as quickly as possible. Their sting is very painful and leaves a red welt as a reminder. Do NOT try to push them away from your area of ascent by sending air bubbles to the surface from your regulator. The bubbles may break off their tentacles and you won't be able to see where the stinging tentacles are. If you are allergic to bee stings, and sea wasps have been spotted at the dive site, consider foregoing the dive as you will most likely have the same reaction to a sea wasp sting.

Stonefish. They may be one of the sea's best camouflaged creatures, but if you receive a puncture from the poisonous spines that are hidden among its fins, you'll know you've found a stonefish. They tend to lie on the bottom on coral, so, unless you are lying on the bottom or on the reef, which you shouldn't be (see "Reef Etiquette and Buoyancy Control"), they shouldn't present a problem. Should you get stung, go to a hospital or a doctor as soon as possible because it can result in severe allergic reactions, and pain and infection are almost guaranteed.

Stingrays. These creatures are harmless unless you sit or step on them. If you harass them, you may discover the long, barbed stinger that is locat-

*A master of disguise, the scorpionfish (*Scorpaena* plumieri) imitates a rock. The venomous dorsal spines can inflict pain and injury if touched. (Photo: J. Schnabel)*

ed at the base of the tail and wields a very painful wound that can be deep and become infected. If you suffer from a sting, go to a hospital or seek a doctor's care immediately. But the best policy is to leave them alone, and they'll leave you alone in return.

Eels. Similarly, eels won't bother you unless you bother them. It is best not to hand feed them, especially when you don't know if other eels or hazardous fish such as barracuda or sharks are in the area. And don't put your hand in a dark hole. It might just house an eel. Eels have extremely poor eyesight and cannot always distinguish between food and your hands. If you are bitten by an eel, don't try to pull your hand away—their teeth are extraordinarily sharp. Let the eel release it and then surface (at the required slow rate of ascent), apply first aid, and then head for the nearest hospital.

Sharks. Although not an extremely common sight for divers, when sharks do appear, it is a cause for celebration and fascination. As a rule, most of the sharks are not aggressive and will not attack divers. However, do not feed them or harass them. If you are unlucky enough to be mistaken for a meal, the nearest hospital is the most logical next stop.

Barracudas. These fish have a miserable reputation. In fact, they are somewhat shy although unnervingly curious. They will hover near enough to divers to observe what they are so interested in, but just try to photograph them and they keep their distance. You'll see them on almost every dive. Don't bother them—and they won't bother you.

Diving Accidents

Diving is a safe sport and there are very few accidents compared to the number of divers and dives made each year. However, occasionally accidents do occur and emergency medical treatment should be sought immediately. If you are diving with a local dive operation, they will be equipped to handle any situation expediently. If a diving injury or decompression sickness occurs when you are on your own, contact a nearby dive operator, the local hospital or clinic, the local recompression chamber (many Caribbean Islands have one now) or call Divers Alert Network at (919) 684-8111. Some of the dive destinations featured in this book are off the beaten track. In some cases, accessibility to a recompression chamber may require helicopter or boat transportation which can be costly—not to mention the cost of chamber treatments. Dive insurance is strongly recommended for every diver.

Divers Alert Network/DAN

This is a non-profit membership association of individuals and organizations sharing a common interest in diving safety. It assists in the treatment of underwater diving accidents by operating a 24-hour national telephone emergency hotline, (919) 684-8111 (collect calls are accepted in an emergency), and increases diver safety awareness through education.

DAN does not maintain any treatment facility nor does it directly provide any form of treatment, but is a service that complements existing medical systems. DAN's most important function is facilitating the entry of the injured diver into the hyperbaric trauma care system by coordinating the efforts of everyone involved in the victim's care.

Calls for routine information that do not concern a suspected diving injury or emergency should be directed to DAN information number (919) 684-2948 from 9 a.m. to 5 p.m. Monday–Friday Eastern Standard time. This number should *not* be called for general information of chamber locations. Chamber availability changes periodically making obsolete information dangerous at the time of an emergency. Instead, divers should contact DAN as soon as a diving emergency is suspected.

Hyperbaric treatment and air ambulance service can be costly. All divers who have comprehensive medical insurance should check to make sure that hyperbaric treatment and air ambulance services are adequately covered internationally. DAN membership includes insurance coverage specifically for dive injuries. Four different membership levels offering four different levels of coverage are available.

Membership ranges from $25–45 a year, which includes dive accident insurance, the DAN Underwater Diving Accident Manual, which summarizes each type of major diving injury and outlines procedures for initial management and care of the victim; a membership card listing diving related symptoms and DAN's emergency and non-emergency phone numbers; decals with DAN's logo and emergency number; and *Alert Diver,* a newsletter that provides information on diving medicine and safety in layman's language. Special memberships for dive stores, dive clubs and corporations are available. The DAN Manual as well as membership information and applications can be obtained from the Administrative Coordinator, National Diving Alert Network, Duke University Medical Center, Box 3823, Durham, NC 27710.

When the infrequent injury does occur, DAN is prepared to help. DAN support currently comes from diver membership and contributions from the diving industry. It is a legal, non-profit public service organization and all donations are tax deductible.

Appendix I: Tourist and Dive Information

Bahamas Ministry of Tourism
800-866-DIVE
305-442-7095

Belize Tourism Board
421 Seventh Avenue, Suite 701
New York, NY 10001
800-624-6686
212-563-6011
Fax 212-563-6033

Cayman Islands Department of Tourism
6100 Blue Lagoon Drive
Miami, FL
305-266-2300
Fax 305-267-2900

Dominica Division of Tourism
P.O. Box 293
Roseau, Commonwealth of Dominica, West Indies
809-448-2045
Fax 809-448-5840

Mexican Government Tourism Office
2707 N. Loop West
Suite 450
Houston, Texas 77008
713-880-5153
Fax 713-880-1833

Saba Tourism and Dive Association
P.O. Box 527
Saba, Dutch Caribbean
011-599-462231
Fax 011-599-462350

Turks and Caicos Tourist Board
Pond Street
P.O. Box 128
Grand Turk, Turks and Caicos, British West Indies
800-441-4419
809-946-2321
Fax 809-946-2733.

Appendix II: Further Reading

Alevizon, Bill, *Caribbean Reef Ecology,* Pisces Books/Gulf Publishing Co., Houston, TX, 1994.

Blount, Steve and Lisa Walker, *Diving and Snorkeling Guide to The Bahamas: Nassau and New Providence,* Pisces Books/Gulf Publishing Co., Houston, TX, 1991.

Collins, Sharon, *Diving and Snorkeling Guide to Roatan and Honduras' Bay Islands,* Pisces Books/Gulf Publishing Co., Houston, TX, 1993.

Cummings, Stuart and Susanne, *Diving and Snorkeling Guide to the Turks and Caicos Islands,* Pisces Books/Gulf Publishing Co., Houston, TX, 1993.

Cummings, Stuart and Susanne, *Diving and Snorkeling Guide to the U.S. Virgin Islands,* Pisces Books/Gulf Publishing Co., Houston, TX, 1992.

Humann, Paul, *Reef Creature Identification,* New World Publications, Jacksonville, FL, 1992.

Humann, Paul, *Reef Fish Identification,* New World Publications, Jacksonville, FL, 1989.

Keller, Bob and Charlotte, *Diving and Snorkeling Guide to The Bahamas: Family Islands and Grand Bahama,* Pisces Books/Gulf Publishing Co., Houston, TX, 1995.

Lewbel, George S. and Larry R. Martin, *Diving and Snorkeling Guide to Cozumel,* Pisces Books/Gulf Publishing Co., Houston, TX, 1991.

Meyer, Franz O., *Diving and Snorkeling Guide to Belize,* Pisces Books/Gulf Publishing Co., Houston, TX, 1990.

Roessler, Carl, *Diving and Snorkeling Guide to The Cayman Islands, 2nd Edition,* Pisces Books/Gulf Publishing Co., Houston, TX, 1993.

Schnabel, Jerry and Susan Swygert, *Diving and Snorkeling Guide to St. Maarten, Saba, and St. Eustatius,* Pisces Books/Gulf Publishing Co., Houston, TX, 1994.

Schnabel, Jerry and Susan Swygert, *Diving and Snorkeling Guide to Bonaire,* Pisces Books/Gulf Publishing Co., Houston, TX, 1991.

Sorensen, Linda, *Diving and Snorkeling Guide to the British Virgin Islands,* Pisces Books/Gulf Publishing Co., Houston, TX, 1992.

Wilson R. and J., *Watching Fishes: A Guide to Coral Reef Fish Behavior,* Pisces Books/Gulf Publishing Co., Houston, TX, 1985/1992.

Index

Bold page numbers indicate photographs.